Into The Afterlife: Paranormal World

Brian Danhausen

Into The Afterlife: Paranormal World

Brian Danhausen Design and Layout by Dark Moon Press

Published by Dark Moon Press

ISBN-13: 978-1502946249

Into The Afterlife: Paranormal World

is published by Dark Moon Press Ft. Wayne, Indiana

For a full catalogue of Dark Moon's publications refer to

http://www.darkmoonpress.com

Or send an SASE and $8.00 to:

P.O. Box 11496, Ft. Wayne, Indiana, 46858-1496

Dark Moon Press

P.O. Box 11496, Fort Wayne, Indiana 46858-1496

Into The Afratic [illegible] World

[illegible] Design and Layout [illegible] Dark Moon Press

Published by Dark Moon Press

Copyright 2014 Dark Moon Press

ISBN-13: 978-1502946249

Into The Afratic [illegible] World

is published by Dark Moon Press, Ft. Wayne, Indiana

For a full catalogue of Dark Moon's publications [illegible]

[illegible]

[illegible] SASE [illegible]

[illegible] Indiana 46859 [illegible]

[illegible]

Table of Contents

Dedication

I would like to dedicate this book to my wife Darlene. She has been by my side through most of these experiences. She has stood by me through all the good times and the bad, even when I have become consumed with all of these things that has happened and I lose my way in all of it. She is always there and able to find a way to guide me back.

Many of the names and locations may not be mentioned by name in these writings due to client and investigator confidentiality. Some of the events also took place at public ghost investigations and may also not be mentioned by name. Stories and tales of ghosts and hauntings are often considered myth and folklore. It is for each individual to decide for themselves on what they may believe or disbelieve, but these are my stories, my experiences that have happened to me during my lifetime. Some taking place on my own and some experiences happening with others, such as my family or my paranormal team that I have founded called, Into The AfterLife Paranormal. All the sketches in this book are done by myself. These are the images of the entities that I have seen during some investigations, and some not on investigations. I am also including some actual photos of evidence caught myself and by team members, past and present of Into The AfterLife Paranormal. I am writing this for several reasons. First, when

I write my experiences down it helps me run them through my head and almost releases them from constant thought. It also helps me to keep track of all that has happened throughout the years. Finally, and hopefully, it will help others who are dealing with similar issues. To possibly understand, or let them know that they are not alone. That there are others out there that deal with the same type of things. To maybe give new theories and thoughts on their situations. You can also view and listen to evidence caught throughout the years at www.intotheafterlifeparanormal.com. Also I will try and include a very brief history on some of the locations, both historical and claims of haunted activity. A lot of the history that I will be adding to the public investigation sections of these writings is based on what I have found on their official web pages.

About the Author

My name is Brian Danhausen, and among other things, I am a paranormal investigator. I say paranormal investigator and not ghost hunter. I do not hunt ghosts, I investigate with the purpose of finding the answers that I seek. Whether it be for myself or a client. I have dealt with the paranormal for most of my life. The experiences that I am about share in these writings were originally written to get what was happening to me clear in my head. Before I started writing them down it was hard to let go of them. They would sit in my head always haunting me, physically and mentally. I also began to paint or sketch the entities that I see. I know that when this first started happening to me I felt "Am I crazy Is this really happening?" So by sharing these experiences now, maybe it will help someone who is experiencing the same things, maybe feel that they are not alone or out of their mind. The difference for me is that I asked to be open. I just did not expect it to come on so strong and so fast but, before I start with my paranormal experiences let me tell you a little about myself.

At the time of writing this book, I am forty two years old and a father of two my daughter Jade and my son Donovan. I am married to my wife Darlene who is also an investigator and will be mentioned throughout these writings. I do have a day job in retail and I am an artist and owner of DarkWynds Mystic Visions. I am also starting a darker art company called

The Final Nail. I have also been in the haunted attraction field for about 20 years now. I have acted, designed, built props and ran many of the attractions throughout the years. Although I have not done any for the past few years, I believe having a background in this helps to explain or de-bunk happenings in the paranormal field. It definitely helps to discover hauntings that may be falsified. Now I do not usually mention this but I am also a practicing Witch. I believe in a God and a Goddess. I commune with nature, the elements and the energies that surround us all. I have been for a great many years. The reason that I mention it now, is because through my teachings and the things that I have learned through the years of practicing the Craft has helped my communication in the spirit world. It has allowed me to open myself and have a better understanding of the things going on around me. Let me tell you this, for a while now I have been slowly trying to open myself up for communication with the spirit world. Several months ago I had opened myself up fully.

Since then, I have been actually seeing the spirits more clearly and also have been able to hear them now. While I still see them physically on occasion, I also now receive pictures and sometimes voices in my mind, and the dreams have become more frequent. Sometimes I do not even need to be in the same room. I know that this sounds off the wall and that most will not believe, and that is fine as long as I do. That is all that matters. I also find myself somewhat acting out what they are doing and trying to communicate to me, and none so much as the two spirits that I encountered in Trinway Ohio. I have visited several of these locations multiple times and some of the events that took place intertwine between locations. So while reading you may find that I will refer back occasionally to the same cases. Also, some of the actual dates allude me as some time has passed and I have just began to actually write my experiences down formally as oppose to chicken scratching on random bits of paper.

And on a few quick side notes, you will notice that the paintings and sketches that I do of the entities have no eyes. This is not to make them scary, it is just the way that I see them sometimes.

The paranormal experiences that I will write about are what has happened to me. I do not claim to be a professional writer or do not claim to have all the answers on anything in the paranormal realm. I do not believe that anyone can. The whole field is a lot of theories and ideas. I believe that is partially why we investigate, not only for answers to our questions, but to find proof to help out our theories. The only way I think that anyone would know anything one hundred percent is, if you yourself were in the afterlife, and I am not even sure that those on the other side know either.

Before I get into my paranormal experiences, I would like to share a few of my thoughts and theories on some subjects. Subjects that may come up in the paranormal field. I must also add, as I will tell all of my clients, I do not guarantee anything in this field. As I do not believe that anyone can, unless you are the one on the other side, and then I am still not sure if they know 100 percent of what is going on. What I will tell my clients is that I will collect the evidence if any compare it to any history found. Then I with all of the data collected, may present a theory on what I believe may be happening at that location. This may also take several different visits and investigations. So again, these are just my opinions and theories that I have come to throughout the years.

I would also like to add this, something that I often tell people when they ask me about this. Imagine this that you and one other person are sitting in a room and nobody else is even close to your location. Then you begin to ask questions into your digital recorder. Now imagine even if at the time, you did not experience anything paranormal. You go to review your audio session and there is a third intelligent answer to one of your questions. There is nothing like it. You know that there were only the two of you, so who is that third voice and why did they answer that particular question? Perhaps they answered them all and that was the only one that was picked up on the recorder. These are some of the answers that I try and seek out. You see for me, that third voice has already shown me that there is something after. Some kind of energy that still exists and seems to be intelligent. Why are they still here? Good question. This is another answer that I seek, why do some stay and some don't.

I would also like to put forth a thought. Why do the entities appear the way that they do? Now remember, this is just a thought, but what if the longer that they are around the more powerful they become. Let say that maybe they go in stages, the weaker ones come across as shadows while the stronger ones are able to manifest into a full body apparition. What if, like when I see them, they seem to be in my head? For example I had seen a full person which I believe was in my head while to other investigators were seeing a shadow block out the laser grid it was same area where I was seeing her.

There are so many questions, answers and theories in the paranormal field and for me, the possibilitics seem endless, and that is in part what makes all of this so exciting.

A Little About The Craft And My Patron Goddess

Of course this is not a book about witchcraft, but being a witch myself, I wanted to include a little background on the subject. As I stated above, as a witch, I deal with nature and the energies that surround us. Which of course would include the energies that come from the afterlife. I also believe that the Divine is the Divine I may call it Goddess and you may call it God or Buddha or whoever, but in the end it is one in the same. I also believe in reincarnation. That we run through our lifetimes until we have learned everything that we need to. When we are done however many lifetimes it takes, some maybe longer and some shorter, we will return to the Divine. In between, we go to the Summer land. This is a place where we can reflect on the lessons of the life just past and plan the ones for the next one. Perhaps, some of these lessons take place in the afterlife. I am also a strong believer in Karma and the Threefold Law. That is whatever you put out into the universe good or bad, you will receive it back in threefold. Anyway, I am what you would call an Eclectic Witch. I take theories and thoughts from all over and apply them to my practices and my way of living. I am open to a lot of different theories and beliefs.

I have learned a theory that once a witch always a witch in every lifetime. It may just take you longer to be awakened. I was awakened by my patron Goddess Hecate. Hecate (or Hekate) is the Goddess of magick, witchcraft, the night moon and ghosts. She is the only child of Perses and Asteria from whom she received her power over heaven the earth and the sea. She is also considered the Goddess of the crossroads and a triple Goddess sometimes depicted with three heads. It is said that three-faced masks also would be placed at the entrances of many homes, honoring the Goddess Hecate, who can wield her influence over "the spirits that traveled the earth" to keep them from entering the household. So to me what better Goddess to have awaken me to the path.

I had been drawing a figure that I had come across in a book for many years before I became a witch. Her name was Hecate. She kept popping up in my life but at the time I did not understand why. When I had begun researching and reading about the craft, many things for me started to fall into place. Including Hecate. Her name kept coming up in everything that I was coming across. In fact, when I bought my first Athame, a ceremonial knife used in ritual, I had three to choose from at the store. I picked one. The shop keep then said "Good choice, Hecate's Athame" I was floored that of the three that I had no knowledge, of I picked Hecate's. From then on, She has guided me through the craft, my life and the paranormal world.

So there is a brief summary and a small bit of background on the subject. I would love to get into more, but that is a whole other book all together.

Hecate

My Theories On Psychic Abilities

Let me start off by saying, that I believe all people have some psychic abilities. It may be it a little or a lot. How many times have you been singing a song and it comes on the radio, or were thinking about a movie and it is on later that night? Some people are just more accepting of them, and some like myself asked to be opened fully. I was taught that why all people have them. There will be an ability that stands out for them, taking the forefront. Such as psychic knowing, seeing, hearing or even smelling. So while the one will come easier, the rest will need to be more developed to enhance them. There are also many different types of psychic abilities. Here is a few examples, you may be a Medium, someone who can communicate with the dead. Or maybe an Empath, and you will pick up feelings and emotions from a person or place.

Please understand though, you do not need psychic abilities to be in the paranormal field or to investigate hauntings. For myself, while I do believe in the psychic ability and feel like it is a tool that can be used during investigations, I like scientific proof to help back it up. While sometimes helpful, I also do not base investigations solely on psychic feelings. I also take care on a case on what I will reveal. I do not wish to influence the investigators or the clients.

When I opened myself. I did a ritual to assist me. I asked for the assistance and guidance from my patron Goddess Hecate. She has guided me through many aspects of my life. She has many dealings with the afterlife as well, so for me, she was the one once again to help me. If you decided to open yourselves, you would want to ask for assistance from someone in your belief system. After asking and performing the ritual, I did not expect it to happen so fast. It was the very next case that my first experience took place. I had to remember though, that this is what I had asked for.

While speaking of opening, I would like to put out there, that before I go into a location, I ground and shield myself for protection. As I believe all paranormal investigators should. Once in the location and I feel ready, I open myself up for communication. This is where you must be most cautious. You do not want an invasion or an attachment or something following you home. You must be the stronger force while communicating, and be in control. If you feel like you are losing control, I would suggest shutting down right away and stepping away from the location. If even for a while until you can regain yourself. Your body and your instincts are your best paranormal tools. Always follow them and always protect yourself. I use grounding and shielding. A lot of people use the White Light shielding. This is when you ask and visualize yourself being surrounded and protected in a white light from the Divine, whoever the Divine may be to you. This is an individual thing and you must find what works for you.

To Know

Ouija VS Modern Paranormal Equipment

I wanted to include my theories on this subject in this book, but wasn't sure where it would fit in. So this spot is as good as any. I am sure that many of you have used or have seen how a Ouija Board works. I myself as a young boy, used to use one in my father's basement which, may have not been the smartest thing to do at the time considering what I know now. I also know that there is a stigma about using one. So here is my question for you all, what is the difference between using a Ouija Board and let's say a digital recorder or even the flashlight for yes and no answers. I have posted this question before on one of my social media sites and had got the argument that you are touching the Ouija Board. That you are using body to help it. Well first, I feel that during paranormal investigations that your body is your best equipment, also there are many times that I am holding my digital recorder while I am asking questions. So in theory aren't we kind of doing the same thing? We are just using a more modern piece of equipment. We are still calling something in that we cannot be 100 percent sure on what it is and we are still opening ourselves up to it. I believe it is not the equipment that you use but your intent and what you say. An object cannot call an entity in, it is the person that is using that object and that person's intent. So with Ouija or modern equipment, either way I would suggest to always try and protect yourself in all of your paranormal activities and you must take responsibilities for doors that you open.

Which reminds me of a case.

A new client called me late on a summer night it was a Friday. She called frantic saying that her and her sister were up in a bedroom of her home. They were messing around with a Ouija Board and something had happened. She went on to explain that it had affected her sister that she thought that it had done something to her. The client explained how her sister glazed over and eyes went black and began talking very strange. She said that she grabbed her sister and fled the home leaving everything were it was. We went out that night. I had requested that the sister come back to the house so that they could close what they had opened. She refused. We looked around the house and saw what was left behind. We set up to come back the next night to see if we could help. The next night I brought the team out. The sister showed up but refused to stay in the house. We did some short sessions to see if there was anything willing to show itself in the house. Nothing was found in review. On a quick side note, I did see a bloody woman in the basement, she was short in size and naked she was trying to tell me something but I have a hard time hearing them. Anyway, as the team was finishing up their sessions, I began to bind the Ouija Board for the clients. I decided to bind because I have always heard that burning will release whatever is in the board into our realm, and breaking it up the same. I used a Pagan binding ritual, well because like I said, I am a Witch. I bound the board and sealed it in a cloth. I handed it to the clients and told them that it was their responsibility to bury it deep within the earth so that no one else would ever find it that was going to be their part in fixing what they had said they unleashed. The last that I heard, she moved from the condo and I have never heard from them again. I do not know if they did what I had instructed them to do and I probably never will.

This next example also shows how some people may over react to a situation. Now I am not saying that they did not experience something in that home, but there was a relative around them feeding them bad information and ideas. So much so that they left the home and all of their possessions behind on the word of that relative saying that all of it was contaminated now because of the Ouija Board. We tried to explain the client that that is most likely untrue and to let us do further investigations to find the true answers, but again, I guess they did what they felt that they needed to do.

Ouija Board

Theory on Possessions and Oppression

We have all seen the movies about people getting possessed. In true life, I believe this would be very rare. To encounter a true demonic haunting or possession in this field would be rare indeed. Now oppression that is a different story. Let's use this as an example, if you worked with someone who was always negative and complaining, after a while you would start to show the same traits and eventually, I believe, become the same way as the person that you are always around. If you had a spirit attached to you always, with you its traits, would affect you in the same way. Eventually, making you the way the entity wants you to be. More of an influence as opposed to possession. If a person was bad in life why would they not be bad in death? It does not make them a Demonic, it just makes them a bad spirit. Which is also not good, but I would believe much easier to get rid of than a demonic presence and more likely what you would come across on an investigation. Now I am not saying that possession does not happen, or that you won't come across it, because you may. I would just suggest not taking on anything that you cannot handle. In a case of possession you are dealing with someone's life, so be certain on what you are dealing with beforc jumping into something that may be potentially dangerous to your clients and yourself.

Here is an example of a case involving someone who claimed to be possessed. We were called by a wife of a man who claimed to be possessed. We went out to do an interview with them. They had claimed to had to have moved several times from their homes because of the paranormal things following them. We pull up to this small single room motel. Let me put it this way, when we pulled up and got out of the truck two elderly gentlemen emerged thinking that we were there to party.

We entered the single room, the man was sitting on the bed. He had just slammed the last sip of his alcohol that he was drinking as we came in. We began to speak to him about what had been going on. He told us about some of the bad times that he was having and said it was because he felt that he was possessed. He was expecting us to give him an exorcism. We tried to explain to him that we were not qualified to do that. He asked us why we came then. I told him to try and help him, to point him in the direction that we thought might help him. He became slightly agitated, but one of our investigators was able to calm him down. We eventually ended up suggesting to him, with him being a religious man, to seek out guidance from a priest and a church to try and focus on getting his life back in order. There was more to the story background on the man, but I will not get into that. He agreed with us and thought it was a great idea. Then thanked us, and we left. This man had some problems, but it was not possession. Even though it ended up not being anything of the paranormal nature, I was just glad that hopefully, we were able to still help him and his family.

Dark Sided

The Feeling

I would like to take this section and explain, the best that I can, on how I feel when I open myself and/or a spirit is present. Before I go into any location I ground and shield myself. When I leave I tell whoever may be there that they cannot follow me or any member of my team. Does this always work? Not all of the time, but most of the time. I begin by finding a quiet place. In my mind, I have these iron gates covered with vines they face a stormy looking sky. I slowly open the gates saying "I am opening myself up for communication with the other side communication only no attachments taking over or following me. It may take a bit before I start to pick up on something or it may happen instantly. When it starts, it kind of goes like this. This weird buzzing comes over me, like a wave of energy. Strongest in the back of my head. The vision of who they are will pop into my head. Now it is has been hard for me to hear what they are saying but it seems like I will feel their emotions and sometimes act out what they are doing. Some things change from time to time. Sometimes a cold sweat or maybe a loss of the things going on around me, but basically this is how it goes. I do not know what it means or why it happens like this, it is just what I have experienced. When I am done, I push whatever may be there out of the gate and then close them in my mind. A red drape then falls as to cover them as well. I suppose this would be a different for everyone meaning that they may have a door instead of a gate or whatever may suit them.

I would also like to add my theory on how they have been presenting themselves to me. When I first started to see them, they were always in shadow form. As I grew and opened myself more the clearer they became. Is it possible that the more open I became the clearer they were? Of course, or could the shadow stage just depend on the strength or stage of the entity? That may be possible as well. Of course there is also the theory that the shadow person is a separate type of entity all together. Any and all of these theories may be possible.

My opening starts my moving a tattered red curtain that reveals a rusted iron cemetery gate. Beyond that lies an old graveyard on a grassy hill. Stormy skies are brewing in the background. I unlock the gate saying " I am opening up myself for communication. Communication only. You may not attach yourselves to me or follow me home." I then open the gate allowing me to, what I perceive to be communication with the dead. When I close, as I mention above, I push everything back court of the gate. When I feel that all is out, I then lock the gates and the curtains fall. Again, this is just my way, everyone else that may do this will find their own ways.

Sketch Of What My Opening Looks Like

Growing Up With the Paranormal

Ever since I can remember, I have always been attracted to the odd movies, toys, stories, all to do with horror monsters and ghosts. As I got older the more my interests grew.

From a young age, I remember dreams of death and the dead. S a side note, the theory is that it is easiest for the spirit world to communicate with us when we are asleep. Our minds are more opened and not restrictive. A theory that I happen to believe.

I would constantly hear what sounded like footsteps in the hall outside my room. Voices would pull me out of that just about asleep state. And that familiar feeling that you are being watched.

The first visual I had ever seen, was a blue steak of light in the hall of the house I grew up in. It was mid-day summer, I believe it was around ten or eleven. It formed before my eyes and shot down the hall towards the bathroom. Of course, being younger, I did not go to investigate, instead I did just the opposite, I left the house very quickly. I never told anyone in the house at that time what I had saw.

Around that same time, a box of facial tissues flew off the top of the TV and landed across the room. Again, I was the only one that had witnessed this. It always seemed to happen when I was alone.

From that point, I began to block the things that were happening to me out. It was not until my teenage years that I began to regain the interest in the paranormal. It started up again. Around the age of fourteen I believe, is when I saw something strange in the sky. This time I was not alone. Myself, a female friend at the time and her friend were standing in the park across from my house talking. Out of nowhere, a perfect triangle flew into the sky above the park. It was hard to determine the size but we could see markings all over it. The triangle flew in stopped in mid-air for what seemed like at least a minute spun backwards a few times and took off at great speed. We all stood there in disbelief. Not knowing what to do next. I mean who would believe, us a bunch of kids.

This kick started my interest back into the paranormal and the experiencces that I had already had.

I began to start reading into anything that dealt with ghosts, UFO's, Cryptozoic and anything that had to do with anything paranormal.

On a side note, anyone that knows me, well knows that the dead I can deal with, but aliens, although I am really interested in, them they really freak me out. I have awoken to a spirit standing beside my bed, which is bad enough, but if it was an alien when I awoke, well I would probably have to change my sheets.

I also began to research many religions. I wanted to know the different opinions on life after death. I grew I knew about that, but I had to read about the others. I read up on the Church, Satanism, Buddhism, paganism, books on voodoo and witchcraft. As I said before, I landed on paganism and witchcraft. Looking back now, back then it was just research, and now well, isn't it funny how things end up.

That lasted a while, but the teenage years took over with the partying turning into the number one focus. Which led to me living on the street when I was sixteen. It is hard to focus on things such as ghosts when you are sleeping in the stairwell of the school in mid-January, in a friend's car or random garage. Most of the focus turning into keeping warm and finding food.

Shortly after that I, ended up living at my fathers and step mothers house. The paranormal would enter my life again. Even before I moved in, there were stories of a little girl that would stand at the top of the stairs. They would see her often. Although I had never see, the girl, I did see a bigger entity. We had built a room in the basement for me to stay in while I was living there. Which by the way, is where we use to play with my dad's and step-moms Ouija board. When we were young we used to use it almost every time we went over there. The room had a bi-fold door, you know the kind that has the slots in it. At night you could see through the slots almost like a dark blue color. My dad worked the night shift and did not return home until around one to one-thirty am. On this particular night for some reason, I could not fall asleep. As I stared at the bi-fold door, I see a black shape a shape of a man between the slots. It was just standing there watching me. I thought it was my father. I began to say, "What?”.... “What do you want?" The shape turned and left. I looked over at the clock it was only twelve-thirty. I just figured my dad got home early and was messing with me. So I get up and go upstairs to see what he was doing. Everyone else was asleep and there was no one around. I looked out the window and my dad’s car was not there, he was still at work. I waited for him to get home and told him what had happened. He told me that all he has seen was the girl. Other things had happened to my family members that had lived there their whole lives. On a family note, later on in life, I had learned that almost everyone in my family has had multiple dealings with the paranormal. It may be a family thing.

Very shortly after that I got back with my now wife Darlene, and even a shorter time than that, we had my son. I was eighteen when he was born. My focus once again shifted from the paranormal to what was going on in my life.

As my son was growing up, I began to get into the haunted attraction field. Designing, building them and props and acting at them. This held my interest for many years. This was also a hard time in my life. I think that I buried myself into that scene instead of facing my problems, but that is a whole other story. Although during this time myself, my wife and my son witnessed these strange lights in the sky and a mass of helicopters surrounding them, but I could not tell you what they were.

Then the shows started. The first one I remember, they would take a group of people and put them in a haunted location. They would then have to do various tasks. I was once again thrown back into it, but this time I was able to witness people investigating. That show ended up being canceled and that was very disappointing. I began to start reading about it again. A few years later, probably the most famous show on paranormal investigating began. It was straight on investigating, a true group to start to learn from. I never missed a show and would always take notes on what they were saying. Many years later, I ended up meeting some of these television personalities and I would just like to say, they were some of the nicest down to earth people that you would ever meet.

My Current Residence

The home I live in now, well most would probably say it is haunted. I do not. I believe that the spirits in my home come and go, that they know that the people in my home are open to communication with them. We are like beacons of light to them. The reason I say this is, I have seen several different entities in my home from shadows moving up and own my hall, to full shadow people, to full body female apparitions. I have also caught several different E.V.Ps (Electronic Voice Phenomenon). From male to female to child. After I had formed my paranormal team, Into The AfterLife Paranormal, and after some investigations, I have also seen things in my home. It usually only last a few days and then they are gone. When we investigate, we do try and protect ourselves and try to keep things from attaching to us. It does not happen often, but sometimes it sill happens. Again, it just goes to show you may think what you are doing is right but nobody knows for sure.

My first experience in my current home happened about a year after we moved in. It happened on a summer afternoon. When I smoked, we did not smoke in the house, so I was hanging out the door in the kitchen. I saw, what I thought may have been the shadow of the mailman walk across my front porch. Didn't think nothing of it. I turned, took a hit off my cigarette and turned my head inward again. The shadow, now in my house, walked out of the wall and headed down my hall. I witnessed this face on no more than ten feet in front of me where my dining room meets my living room. I could not believe my eyes. I told my wife when she got home, but I am not sure if she believed me.

It was quiet for a long time before the next encounter. The next encounter happened with myself and my daughter. We were sitting on the couch which faced the hallway. I was tying my shoe, getting ready to take my daughter to school kindergarten. She was sitting next to me. Out of the top of my eye, I saw a black mass in the hall. It was there for a second and shot down the hall. Just as I am sitting there thinking I am crazy, my daughter says "Daddy did you see that?" I asked what she saw, as she saw it dead on. She said she saw a cat walking backwards down the hall. Maybe a cat is what she said because it resembled a cat to her, I do not know for sure. Myself thinking ghost. I asked her what color it was. I was expecting her to say your average ghost color of white, but she said black. Which to me confirmed me that I was not just seeing things. On another side note, my daughter once told us she saw a pilgrim man standing in the kitchen. I once again told my wife, but still had the feeling she did not quite believed what was happening. Soon she would.

My wife Darlene's first experience that I know, of happened one early morning while she was getting ready for work. I do want to put this out there, it was a hard time for the family, and I am not positive if this had anything to do with her encounter or not, but I like to believe it did. My dog a black lab named Kane, after thirteen years, died in our home. Darlene, as well as the rest of the family was torn up. Darlene woke up and proceeded to walk to the bathroom to get ready for work, she reached down to pet Lucy, one of our three dogs who is also a black lab. As she reached down, her hand kept going into nothing. There was nothing there. Lucy was in the bedroom still. After this, Darlene began to experience more and more things. Enough to peek her interest in the paranormal field. Around this time is when we started to buy equipment and went to our first investigation. We went with friends to a very famous reformatory in Ohio and shortly after that we went solo to a famous fort in Detroit. We were hooked, but we will get into that in a bit. This is also when I started to run the equipment in my house.

Now just to be clear, the occurrences in our home will happen in spurts. We may go many months without any activity. Suddenly it will pick up, sometimes after investigations, which I may be able to understand, and sometimes just out of nowhere. I do not understand why it happens like this, but after speaking to several people who have activity in their homes, it is quite often the same. It comes and goes.

Me and Darlene used to sit in the living room and watch shadows and lights moving up and down the hallway. Listen to weird noises and one night I was basically asleep, Darlene woke me up and told me to look at the door. It was closing by itself. I was in awe, she threw a pillow in front of the door to stop it from closing. We got out of bed to inspect it. We could not explain why it was shutting by itself.

As the years go by, I have had more intense encounters. Besides the pictures that I have also caught in the house, I have also caught many E.V.P.'s. This is the story of the first. I was laying on the love seat, which ran parallel with the kitchen. I was watching, of course, a ghost hunting show. I turn my head and look into the kitchen. My heart starts to pound. as I realize what I am staring at. Standing behind the refrigerator is a full shadow person. It is sticking out about half way, in a half crouch, hands on knees. It seemed like an eternity that we had a stare down. As soon as I was able to snap out of it, I jumped up. At that instant, the shadow person took off toward the sink area, which is a dead end. I ran into the kitchen and nothing was there. I searched for my camera, but found my digital recorder on the TV. I grabbed it and went into the kitchen and turned on the recorder. I began to ask questions. I made a statement that if whoever was there wanted to speak into the red light, I could hear them later. I paused for an answer and suddenly got the chills. Now I state this on the recording, and here is the thing, during the playback, at the pause, I caught a whisper saying, "No". This sent a chill down my spine. I think it was a mixture of disbelief, excitement and perhaps even a little bit of fear. It is so much more different when you actually capture evidence in your home than just suspect it. I went and woke my wife to show her, who response was too, disbelief.

Sketch of the "Kitchen Peeker" entity

Another encounter took place late one night. I was downstairs in the basement getting my stuff for work the next day. That is when this chain of events started to take place. As I gathered up my clothes, I saw what seemed to be a shadow run down the wall of the laundry room. I ran in there to see what it may be. After about a half a minute of being in there, from the other part of the basement, the snare drum belonging to my sons drum set tapped twice. I went out there and jumped around it as to try and recreate it, it was not the same. The spring underneath would make a noise, but not the tapping sound that I had heard. Excited, I ran upstairs to share what had just happened to Darlene, who was in bed under the covers with one of the dogs over her legs. After explaining what happened, I went out to lock up for the night. As I chained the front door, I turned to see a figure in my hall. For about a second I thought it was Darlene, messing around with me. As I stepped towards it, the being took off down the hall. I ran after it immediately. To my surprise, as I reached the bedroom, Darlene was still in bed under the covers with the dog on her legs.

Sketch Of the "Hall Peeker" that I thought was my wife Darlene

Although I cannot pinpoint exact dates on when these experiences happened, I am going to include them in this section. Several times since I have lived in this house, my guess would be at least 5 to 6 times, I have had a shower visitor. Yes, I know that sounds funny, but when you are in the shower and there is something else in the room with you, not so fun. There have been times when I have heard shuffling or talking in the room. Other times I would see something peek quickly from the far side of the shower curtain or from above the curtain rod. Most of these times, I had thought it to be Darlene messing around with me, but every time I would look out of the curtain instantly and there would be no one in the room. One time I even called her in to tell her what had been going on.

The next occurrence took place in the morning, now at this point I put down the rule for the entities that visit my home, that they must not enter any of the bedrooms, especially when we are asleep. I awoke about seven am, it was summer and daylight was in the house. My bed faced, as to see down the hall. A shape as tall as the ceiling and blocking out the pictures that hang on the wall. Stood there, solid black figure, staring at me. Again, once I realized what I was looking at, my heart began to pound. After a few seconds of the stare down, my daughter jumps out of her room and shouted "Good morning daddy!!!" I just about had a heart attack. Now my daughter never saw this entity, as it was behind her and fled towards the living room when she jumped out.

Sketch of the Hallway Entity

I have seen things shoot down my basement stairs. As a matter of fact, one night Darlene was standing on the landing looking at the moon out the back door. Suddenly she got very uneasy as she felt like something was coming up the stairs after her. She quickly came up the stairs and told me right away. Shortly before this experience, she had a dream of a man named Jimmy, standing on the stairs smoking. I myself caught several E.V.P.'s down there, but the one that stands out to me the most was of a child not a man. The E.V.P. was very quick and hard to understand, but when I put it in the computer, I was able to slow it down. "I will play with you" is what it said.

This next story is a little more bizarre to me. I awoke one morning, once again to see a shadow person standing in my bedroom door. As I sat up, it took off. I went and got my digital recorder and began my session. I asked for a name, as usually do at the beginning of my sessions. The name "Tom" comes through as a whispery voice. Now here is the bizarre part, no more than a week before that, my neighbor died at his job. His name was Tom. Could this be the same Tom that answered my question? Maybe trying to get a message to his family? I cannot be sure. I went back after listening to it and started another session, but I got nothing else.

This next story will intertwine with locations that I will speak about later. These parts had just happened at my home.

The dream. I did not know the meaning of this dream at the time. I did not understand what it meant, until we arrived and heard the history of an investigation we were going to a week later. The investigation was at a Manor in Pennsylvania. I originally thought this location was an insane asylum, but then learned at the end of its run, it was a care facility for the elderly and looking like a hospital. In the dream, I was in a hospital setting, it had been closed for at least a few years. There were still gurneys and hospital equipment in the halls.

Suddenly, I was swarmed by what seemed like hundreds of people, a lot of them older. They were all screaming and yelling at me. I said to them "Please, one at a time, I cannot hear you all at once." I awoke still feeling off. I step out in the hall to use the bathroom. I have never felt so claustrophobic in my life. I went into the bathroom and the feeling left. As I stepped back into the hall, the feeling returned. I told them they all have to leave, that there are too many of them. I got back in bed and was still seeing shadows in the hall. Now this next part will really sound weird and I will talk about this entity soon. A big white entity had been following from case to case. I did not know if it was an attachment or what, but on this particular night the entity appeared again and blocked the doorway as to not let the hospital people on to my room. I am still trying to figure that one out.

This is a short occurrence. I have only seen these two on this one night. Again, I awoke in the middle of the night and went into the restroom. It was a stormy night. I looked out the bathroom window and saw standing, in my backyard, and in the rain, was a woman and a little girl holding hands. The woman was dressed in white, but I could not see her face. The young girl was in a yellow rain jacket covered in blood. I stared at them for a brief moment did a double take and they were gone.

Sketch of the Two Entities That Were Standing In My Yard

The adult woman appeared to be headless and much harder to see. Perhaps from an accident. I am not sure, but that was the feeling that I got from them.

We did an investigation in Allegan Michigan, at the Allegan Lodge. For about two days after, I was seeing shadows throughout my home. So I decided to do a spirit box session. Now for those who do not know, a spirit box is a radio that has been altered to scan through the channels very quickly. You still may here bits of words and signals coming through, but if you can get a full word, or even better, a full sentence, you may be speaking to someone in the afterlife. If it is answer to a question you have asked, even better. Anyway, the first session I did I did not pick up anything. The second however,

I ask where did you come from, my answer "Allegan" a direct answer to a question. After that the shadows disappeared.

The final story that I will be sharing from my current home is not a long one, but is probably the one that has affected me the most. My grandmother had breast cancer. She had taken the treatment and was well for many years. She fell ill again, and it was not going good. One night I awoke from a dream that I was having. My grandmother, who was with my great grandmother had come to me in my dream. They were speaking to me, but I could not hear them I pleaded with them to repeat themselves, but they turned and walked away together. I woke my wife Darlene up and had to tell her. I proceeded about my daily tasks. When I got home from work that day I received a phone call from my father. He said I had better sit down. I told him, before he said anything else that I already knew. My grandmother had passed away. Even now as I write this it affects me and it probably always will.

So, I was in the midst of writing the section of this book about some Ohio investigations when I had to stop and come back to this section. I awoke from a dream last night, this one was different. I could hear what the spirit was saying.

It started at a haunted location, a house that I do not know as of yet. As I was standing there a bathroom door, white and the paint chipping away, it closed by itself. I asked if it was a spirit, to please open the door. It did. I asked a few more times and each time it worked. Now as I am sure many investigators will agree with me, to get something to happen on command is rarer than you may think. Anyway, back to the dream. I was astonished. Just then, I began to pick up on a boy. It was a younger boy who was moving the door. I asked him "Why are you being so cooperative now?" He replied "Because THEY want to know more about you", and I said "Who are THEY?" Reply "THEY are the ones who watch over us.", "But who are THEY?" I questioned again. The boy answers "I am not sure, we cannot see THEM." Just then, I felt a presence in the dream, a stronger presence. The feeling that I was getting from it was, that the boy was saying too much and it was there to stop it. That is when I awoke. I thanked the boy aloud for being so open to me. I was asleep for less than an hour when I had this dream and when I did wake up, the strangest feeling was looming in my house.

This blew my mind. What was the meaning of this dream? Is there a hierarchy in the spirit world? Ones that watch over the spirits on Earth? Higher up than them, but lower than the Divine? Why can they not see THEM? Is it like us not being able to see the spirits that haunt the Earth? Well, not see them for the most part. Were they my Guardians or something more? I will approach my next EVP session with some new questions for sure. This dream has opened up a whole new view for me to explore. This is definitely a topic that I will explore further as I continue in the paranormal field.

Yet another dream has happened during the writing of this book. This time in the dream, I was investigating with another team. The house was old and had a green tone just like in the dream before. I will have to check into the meaning of that. I was talking to a large man. If I remember correctly he was laying on a table. I turned to see a full shadow figure, it ran up the stairs. I could then hear the footsteps running across the ceiling. I talked about it to the other team. That is all that I can remember about the dream at this time.

November 17th 2013: A man in a trench coat, with sort of spiky hair is standing at my screen door. Eyes as black as the night. It is unseasonably warm today and raining. The time is about 5:35pm. I did not invite him in. I do not know who it is. I told him that maybe later we can talk, he gave me the OK sign and walked away. I guess we will see later if he returns.

Nothing more from the entity mentioned above, but a few days later I was at an investigation and one of the investigators fell down the stairs and got hurt pretty bad. Not really sure what happened or why, and I am not saying that had anything to do with it. It was just weird. Perhaps it was a warning.

So this will be the second time that I will write about this dream. The first one for some reason disappeared off my computer. The day started off by seeing a white shadow move through my dining room to my basement stairs. By the way, this was towards the end of December, before Christmas. I had fallen asleep on the couch. In the dream, an invisible being was for some reason trying to take out my left eye. I was fighting it, trying to hold my eye in. I could feel the pain and the burning in my eye in the dream. I was screaming at it to stop. I awoke yelling at the entity to leave. My hand was over my left eye pushing down on it as to hold it in. It was burning like in the dream.

So now it is January 4th 2014, a new year, but I am starting to see a pattern. During the day I felt a presence lurking in the hallway. I also once again fell asleep on the couch. The dream: I was with my wife in a van, the snow was very deep. A white dog was circling the van and from time to time would jump on the hood to the roof. It even bit a guy in the knee walking down the street. We then do an E.V.P. session, but I cannot remember what it says. Maybe this dog was trying to keep me in the van, protect me from the house that we were going into investigate. I am not sure. Anyway, we somehow end up in the house and started setting up equipment in the basement. I felt a dark force. The darkest that I have felt. A force then pushes me up against the basement wall. Some weird black mass engulfs me and then it feels like I am being bricked into the wall. Somehow I get out and up the stairs.

Myself and Darlene end out back in the van. I fall asleep in the dream and then awake screaming in the dream. I do not know why, but in the dream something scared me almost to death. I was trying to scream in the dream, but I could not get a sound out. Now I really awoke my throat was so dry and I was choking. Once I was able to grasp my breath back. I noticed the same feelings that I was having in the dream. This is the first time in a long time that I have felt uneasy in my home. I wrote down what I had dreamt about and went into the bedroom. It took me a long time to get back to sleep as I felt the entity watching me from my bedroom door.

Here is something weird. As I am writing this, I get a text from my wife Darlene, who is at work and I have not talked to her yet. She tells me that she had a dream last night about a ghost boy. It ends up being at the same time that I was dreaming. Her dream starts off with a blue and black energy in the hallway and it goes into the living room. She tells it that it is being annoying and needs to show itself. It turns into a pig. It then reverts back into the energy. She says it again and it turns into a boy about ten years old with dirty blonde hair. She says that they are now on the couch. She has to tell it that she belongs to me we are together. As if it believes that they are together. That's how she describes it to me. She also told it that it had to stay away from my daughter. Then, somehow Darlene's relatives who are still alive entered the dream. She does not remember much else, accept that it was snowing in her dream and something about fish eating worms when the entity was a pig.

Here is the pattern that I have been seeing as of late. I see something during the day, I fall asleep on the couch. I dream, or assume I am dreaming of being attack by an unseen force. Here is the significance of falling asleep on the couch. I always tell the spirits that visit my home that they are not allowed in any of the bedrooms, thus is why I believe they are always standing outside my bedroom door. Anyway, by sleeping on the couch, I am starting to feel like I am leaving myself open to them and they are messing with me while I am asleep. Why does it seem like they are attacking me? I do not know at this point. I guess the answers will come to me when it is time.

So it is still January 4th 2014 about 8:30 pm. I was in the shower washing my hair. I opened my eyes to see a gray humanoid mass staring at me from behind the shower curtain. For a split second I thought it was Darlene my wife, but at this point I know better. It stayed for about two to three seconds and fled moving the shower curtain. I quickly looked out into the bathroom, but nothing or no one was there. This is not the first time I have seen things in the bathroom peeking over the shower curtain, speaking or walking around while I am in the shower. I think that I push these experiences to the back of my mind. They are almost as bad as waking up to having something staring at you.

January 14th around 11pm: Lying in bed, my wife Darlene rolls over and looks at me "I think there are things in the hallway." I reply by saying “I know.” She then says "No. I see them sometimes but it feels like there is always something in the hall." I once again reply that I know, and the conversation was over.

January 26th 9:23 pm: Working on the computer when I look up to see a black mass floating in the dining room. Actually it looked more long and swirly than anything. As I saw it, it took off towards the sink area. Nothing was in there when I went in after it. **10:37** I am standing in the kitchen facing the microwave. I hear three distinct footsteps walk up behind me. I turn and there is no one there. A shiver goes down my spine. I head to the bedroom to see where my wife Darlene is to find her covered in bed. As of late, I have been feeling very uncomfortable in this house. I also wonder how many more paranormal events will take place while writing this book. It also seems to me to be somewhat of a delay. You see every time I try to go back and write from one of the cases or hauntings, I must keep coming back to write in this section. Or, is it something that followed us home from the case in Hazel Park, Michigan that we had done the night before

January 31st: 6:56pm: Darlene went down the basement stairs to grab some laundry. She froze as she saw a misty white light floating there. It went away, she took another step and it was there again at the bottom of the stairs and then gone again. She came and told me and grabbed the dogs to go back downstairs with her.

March 1st 2014: 12:30pm: I was talking with a friend who was interested in joining the team. I have worked with her before and she is very trustworthy. She is also a much more experienced medium than myself, if that is even what I am. I have not ever spoken to her about the activity in my house detail wise. As we were talking shop, she looks at me and asks me if I know that there is a very tall man in my house. I said yes. There are many that pass through this house. She then tells me that he is in the hall. I then proceed to tell her about the tall shadow figure spoken about earlier in these writings. She then proceeds to tell me that he is there to help the others pass through my house, but he is grumpy. A few minutes later, she says there is also a chubby man here, but he is just passing through. Kind of backed up what my thoughts are about my current home.

March 2nd 2014: 10:30pm: I was laying reversed in my bed watching the television. For an odd reason, I look over at my bedroom door. A black mass, not touching the ground, floated into the room blocking out the reflecting doorknob. It then disappeared. I jumped up and told it that it was not allowed in any of the bedrooms. Nothing else was seen. Now this maybe a coincidence, but once again I awoke choking in my sleep 2:00am.

March 17th 2014: 10:27pm: I was locking up for the night to go to bed. As I turned the T.V. off I looked up. In front of the doorway, in the kitchen stood a taller shadow figure. Not as tall as some that I have seen in this house, but a good size. I adjusted my eyes to make sure that what I was seeing was what I was seeing. I stepped forward to approach it. It was weird this time. There was no racing heart when I realized what it was. Maybe I am getting used to it. Anyway, as I stepped towards the kitchen, it took off toward the sink area. I turned on the dining room light and looked around, but there was nothing. As I am typing this, a thought ran through my head. Myself and Darlene had just got back from spending a weekend at a haunted prison in Ohio. We slept in the prison for both nights and of course, had investigated. So I started to wonder if something followed us back. Now this is a place with the type of entities that you would probably do not want to follow you, being possible criminals and all. Here is what popped in my head, what if whoever it was, is waiting for me to review my evidence, to make sure that I get whatever message that it gave me during our investigation. I guess we will see when I review if anything came through.

March 18th 2014: 10:30pm: Well the shadow figure was back again tonight. I am only guessing that it was the same one as the night before. I got in bed and changed the channel on the television. As I turned to lay my head down, I saw it standing in the door. It stood for but a few seconds and took off towards the living room. There was no further activity that night.

March 30th 2014: I had just returned from a case at a historic house in Royal Oak Mi. I ended up falling asleep on the couch again. Within a few moments I was almost asleep. A very loud female voice shouted my name right in my ear. It awoke me instantly. I told her to please stop doing that. I soon fell back asleep. For the rest of the night, I kept having choppy dreams of the house a lot of details are hard to remember, but I remember the rooms and many entities in the house, it felt very crowded. I awoke in the morning feeling very flustered. I soon shook it off and went about the day.

April 7th 2014: 10:37pm: This was a fast experience, but I thought that I would include it because it was pretty profound. I had just gone to bed and was laying there watching T.V. I could see the light from my daughter's bedroom through the crack of her door. I started seeing a black mass block out and move across the door. At first I thought it was her shadow from inside her room. I could not hear her moving around. I continued to watch T.V. and every few seconds it would happen again. The last time I had seen it though I caught it straight on. It was darker than the dark hall and I could tell that it was on my side of the door. I then saw a quick dot of light underneath the black mass. As I looked down as to be distracted by the light, the black mass took off down the hall toward the living room.

Usually I would chase these things, but I feel as of late that I am becoming more accustomed to them in my home. Perhaps too accustomed.

It is still **April of 2014,** I have been seeing a lot of shadows this month. I do not know why, but it seems that every few days I will see a shadow and then it takes off.

May 4th 2014: The night after the team did the cleansing at the Southfield, Michigan case. Once you read the Southfield, Michigan case later in these writings, I mention about the weird death images that were I feel placed in my head by the entity in the home. Well the dream that I had this night was very reminiscence of some of the images that I was seeing during that investigation. This was probably the strangest dream that I have ever had. This was also a very choppy dream.

The Dream: It started in a scene of which seemed to be after the worlds end, after some horrific war or something. I was with an older man. I do not know who he was. We were riding motorcycles through the desolate land. We reached a make shift civilization. There they were cooking some meat. In the dream, I knew that there was no meat left that was not contaminated. A man approached and said "Where is my son?"... "Oh there he is, cooking." Not cooking the meat, the son was the meat and he was OK with it. We were on foot now, as we reached the end of what seemed to be a corridor. As we sat at a table, I told the man that we had to get out of there. That they were probably going to use us as meat. As I searched for a way out, I came across a room with a bunch of younger people in it. The center of their heads were gone. Something was eating their brains but they were still alive. Their faces were blank, but horrific looking with blood running down from the opened wounds. The tall shadow man from the Southfield Mi case was in the corner of the room. Just then, I had realized that it had been watching me during the whole dream. As I seen him, I awoke.

I thought strongly about not including this dream just because of the bizarre nature of it, but I do believe that it had something to do with the cleansing, so there it was.

Sketch from the dream that I had after the Southfield Case

Saturday Morning May 24th 2014: I have started to notice something within these last few weeks. A new possible theory that I would like to share. We had two cases on tap a few weeks ago. As soon as they were booked, I started seeing the black shadows again. At first out of the corner of my eye, but then dead on. Unfortunately, both cases ended up canceling. As soon as that happened, the shadows disappeared. A few days ago I was contacted by my sister, whose house we have investigated before. Her activity had picked up once again. I booked it for an investigation on the date above. The day I booked it, the shadows returned. I have been seeing them every day since the booking. It seems that almost every time I turn around I see a fleeting shadow taking off. So the theory is, are these the spirits from the cases that I book? I am starting to think that they are. If it is possible for them to follow you home, why not visit prior. For what reason, that I am still working on. Perhaps to greet us or even to scare us away, depending on the entity that you are dealing with. I do believe, as I mentioned before, that they know when we are coming and what we do, that we are like beacons to them. I also believe that they know that we are the ones that will communicate with them. So why wouldn't they come to us investigators of the paranormal.

May 31st 2014: We had just spent the day at the Paranormal Gathering in Bath Mi. This was a site of great tragedy that you will read about later in the "Paranormal Unity" section. Another dream. In the dream, I was being led around by a young girl. She held my hand and was dragging from location to location in this building. It was in a city and a very tall, business type building. It seemed that after every room, that we had just left, exploded. Even after we took the elevator to exit the building, it exploded as well. There was a woman there that we had tried to warn, but she did not listen and died. She was but one of many that perished in these multiple explosions. We ended up outside and watched as the building burned. She was then gone and I woke up. Now, was this dreaming just the influence of the location and story of Bath MI? Possibly, but I have been getting better at distinguishing a "normal" dream compared to a "visitor" dream, as I call them. In the visitor dreams, things seem very real and you can actually feel the connection and the emotions of said visitor. It is a little hard to explain, but there is a difference. Even as I am writing this, twice I have had to stop as dizziness came over me. I do not know why, it was just weird.

July 1st 2014: I have been back from the Waverly Hills trip for almost two weeks at this point. I have been seeing the shadows popping in and out of the walls of my home. Nothing dead on though, but more than just out of the corner of my eyes. It is more like just out of the line of sight.

July 8th 2014: 10:45 pm I was laying in my bed watching a cooking show. From the corner of my eye, I caught something bright standing in my doorway. At first I thought it maybe headlights shining through, even though my curtains are almost always closed. As I turned my head to take a look, I knew that it was no headlights. It appeared to be a bright white and the form looked and I felt female. I watched for just a few seconds, if that, and it took off towards my living room. I immediately jumped out of my bed and shot down the hall. There was nothing there. I asked what it had wanted, but received no answer. This on seemed odd to me, only because this was the first time that I had seen something in this form usually it is a shadow being or much more detailed in its form. Never has been a glowing white. I wonder what it means.

Sketch of the White Entity from the hallway

Sunday August 10th 2014: This was my first night back after being at a paranormal convention for 4 days in the Upper Peninsula. Finally, in my own bed, I begin to drift. In my head, I see it the tall shadow man that I have seen before standing in the hall. I am not 100% that this is the same one, but that was the feeling that I had got, and feel that it was. He came out of the hall closet area and stood in my bedroom door. It seemed like he was there for a while and trying to tell me something, but I do not know what. He remained to stand there, and after what seemed like a few minutes, I popped up in my bed. I looked out the door and nothing was there. The time had only lapsed about ten minutes since I had layed down to go to sleep.

The next few pages shall show some photos I have caught, these are actual photos from my home:

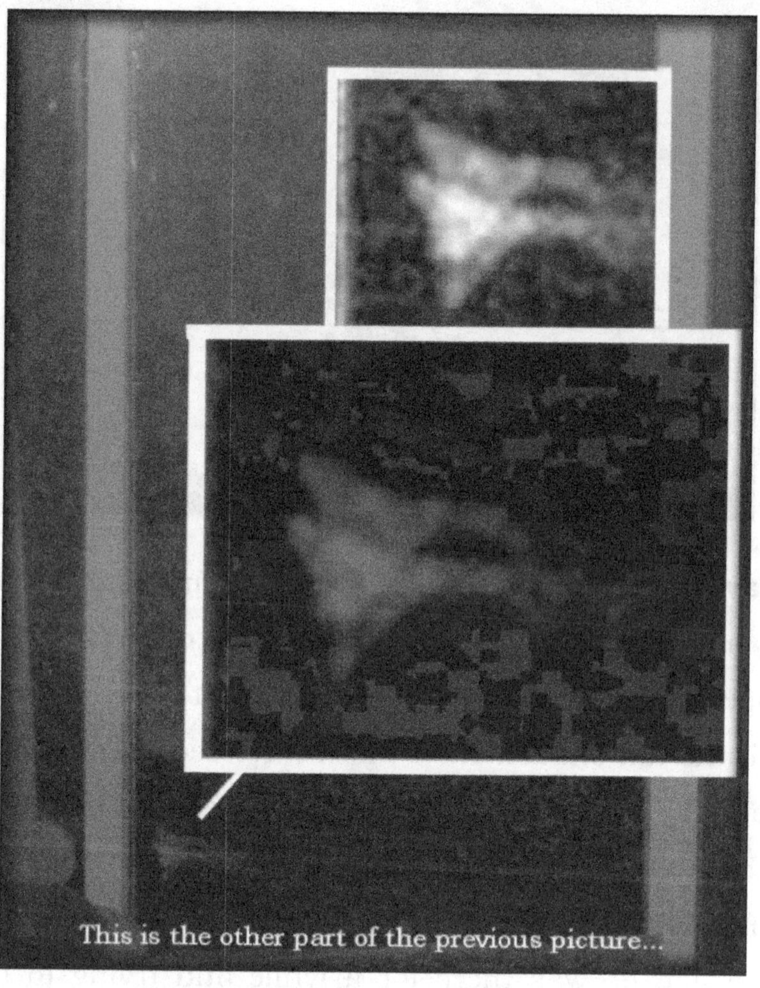
This is the other part of the previous picture...

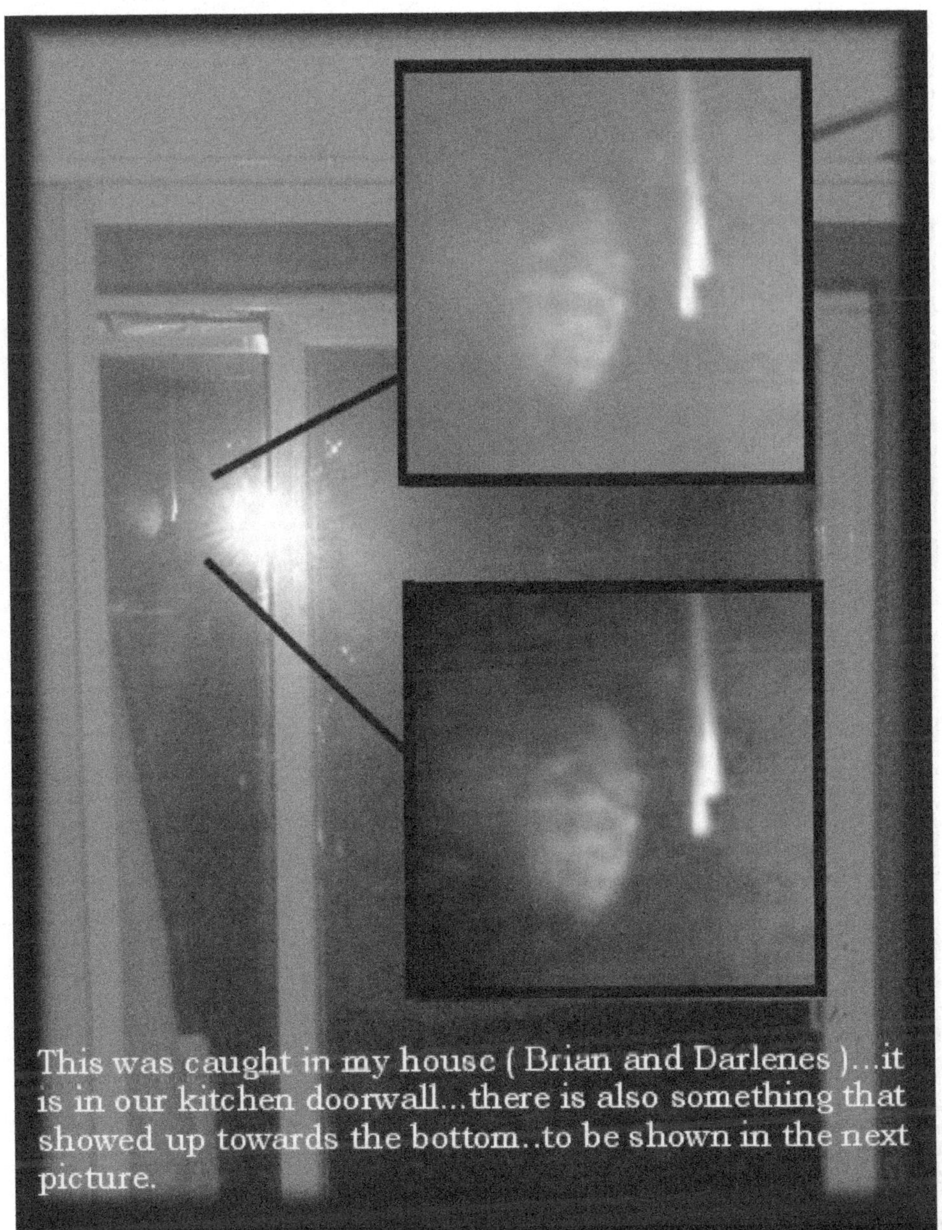

This was caught in my house (Brian and Darlenes)...it is in our kitchen doorwall...there is also something that showed up towards the bottom..to be shown in the next picture.

This one is a little harder to see...same area in the hall... but shot on a different day...still looks female to me.

In The Family

I have come to feel that it is not just myself in my family that has been experiencing the paranormal. As I had mentioned above, in my fathers and step mothers house, there was activity. There was a shadow man that I saw in the basement and the little girl at the top of the stairs. To add to that, I remember a story that my sister had told me. She had kept nail polish on a shelf in her room, it was of course, sealed tight. She witnessed it move off the shelf as it spilled on the floor, the lids unscrewed. Was this a ghost? I cannot say, it was just strange. I do know that she feels that they follow her as well. Another thing that I found odd was this. When she was looking for a house to buy, she would ask if anyone had ever died in the home. Every house that she looked at this was asked, except the one that she ended up purchasing. For some odd reason, she had forgot to ask. An old man that had lived in the house had passed away in the front bedroom.

She had started to experience activity in the home. Seeing and hearing things. This was during the time that I was doing the leg work for the team, but she had asked us out to investigate. We took what little equipment that we had, and investigated. We did capture some strange E.V.P's. In fact, one of them was the last name of the man that had passed in the home, along with some female voices.

A long while after, she had asked us to come again. She had felt that the activity had begun to increase. At this time we had most of the newer team in place. We were going to do a full blown investigation. Funny thing, all of the team except me and Darlene fell ill or could not make it that night. We decided to still go. We got there and it seemed peaceful. The only thing that happened that night was this. I had set an EMF detector in the hallway. We did do a prior sweep of the whole house for EMF's. I was doing a session in the front bedroom, when suddenly the meter began to beep. I went out to see what it was and nothing was there. I picked it up and began to move it around, it did not go off again. I went and joined Darlene in the living room. After a while, it went of again. Much more briefly this time. I went to check it again still nothing. We did not capture any other evidence that night, audio or visual. Although the meter was cool, I could not present that as evidence of a haunting by itself. With that though and the audio evidence from before, it is starting to build the case.

There was one of the other incidents that had happened there. This was before we had gone out again. It was in the front bedroom, where at this time, she had a roommate living in there. We were over there for the holidays. I had gone down to the restroom. As I entered the hallway, I got that feeling. The feeling of being watched. Then the feeling of a presence began to form. I could see him sitting on the edge of the bed in the front room. He was an older man, but the rest of his features were hard to make out. I went and told her what I had seen. This is when we scheduled the return investigation.

When I had contacted my brother about the team, we had begun talking about experiences and how he too had been dealing with the paranormal for a lot of his life. After a time of investigating together, he proceeded to tell me that in his current residence at the time, the family was experiencing strange things.

We were at his home doing and evidence reveal with the team. I had gone upstairs. I entered the living room and saw him in the hall. It was an old man, bald with short white hair on the sides of his head. He was a little plumper and wore a tan button up sweater. I went back downstairs and told them that I had seen something. They had told me that one of the family members had seen a man in the hall. I told them to stop. I would have Darlene text them the description of who I had saw and they would text me the description of who the family member had saw. We did this at the same time after we had got home. I wanted to do this to validate what I had seen. The two sightings in the hall had matched. We had both basically seen the same old man.

My daughter since a young age has also had paranormal experiences. Mostly visual.

My family members have had other things that had happened in their lives paranormal wise, but those are their stories to tell. These are just some of the ones that I have experienced with them. Also, some small examples of how the paranormal runs through my family.

May 24th 2014: Tonight the team will go to investigate my sister's home again. We have been there twice. The first time we had caught phenomenal evidence, the second, although we had a few experiences, no physical evidence was caught. That just goes to show that how at the same location, at different times, how the activity may increase or decrease. Now with the activity increased I am anxious to see what will happen tonight.

So we go out to investigate. Six team members including myself. We set up the equipment as usual. Once the equipment is good to go and before we start the first session, I step out of the room. I go off by myself to open. As I start my opening ritual, as explained before, I pull back the red curtain to reveal the gate that I use to open. Standing there is the Black Shadow Man from the Southfield case. The one that was trying to get into my head, at that case you will read about it later in this book. I try to push it back so that I can try and open, but it just paces back and forth in front of the gate in my mind. I then decide that it is probably a good idea not to open. So I then proceed to grab the investigators to start. We begin with the whole group in the living room. Throughout the session I did have some of the feelings of multiple entities watching us. More so from afar, watching to see what we were doing. A short while in, we began to run the Spirit Box and we were getting some pretty good direct answers. Some of the investigators said that they felt like they could feel something in the room next to them. One of them then became sick to the stomach and had to leave the room. Then eventually the house for a short bit. We ended that session and took a break. I sat at the DVR. As I was talking to my sister, I notice the Ghost Meter go off in the hallway where I placed it. There are claims of hearing footsteps walking up and down the hall all of the time. I yelled out to the remaining investigators still in the living room. They did not here it go off. When it is activated it lights and makes a beeping sound. Perhaps it did not beep, but this is the second time that I have investigated there that this meter has gone off in the hall. I once again went to check to see if anything would set it off, once again nothing did. I gathered up the team for the second session. This time I brought both the home owners to sit in. We more or less talked this session. Sometimes, that is when you get your best evidence, when you are not paying attention. As I sat on the couch facing the hall, I kept seeing a black shadow popping out from the hall. That is when I decided to move into the front bedroom. This is where the old man had died in the house and where I had seen him previously sitting on the bed. Only five of us ended up in the bedroom, one being my sister. We once again ran the Spirit Box. At one point, the investigator holding the box asked a question and it responded by saying her name. She handed off the Spirit Box to the investigator beside her and stepped out of the room. I went to check on her finding her outside with another investigator. She was OK. It was this was the first time that she had her name spoken from a possible entity. I know the feeling, the first time I heard my name spoken, well it is a little freaky. She gathered herself up and we went to rejoin the session

About this point I tried once again to open and once again the Black Shadow Man was there. So once again I did not open myself. We rejoined the bedroom session and once again one of the investigators was feeling off and had to remove herself from the home. We ran a little bit longer and decided to end it. We wrapped up and left for the night. At this point we still have evidence to review but almost all of us had some sort of personal experience happen to us.

Sketch of the Old Man sitting on the bed from my sister's house

Sketch of the Old Man that I saw from my brother's house

The White Entity

The next thing I will speak about is the White Entity. Now this will be out of order. You see this entity is a more recent occurrence, but being as it shows up at other locations that I have investigated at, I figured that I will share the story now. That way you will have the background on it for when it shows up later in these writings.

Now, the first encounter with this entity took place at a location that we have investigated a great many times. Let me be perfectly clear on this next point. I strongly believe that this entity has absolutely no connection to this location. It just happened to be the place it decided to show itself to me.

My team was down at the fort located in Detroit. Like I had said before, we have investigated there many times. This time for me, would be different.

We were all in the barracks building third floor. At first it had seemed quiet. I went into a separate room to try and open myself to anyone who was there. After a short time, I began to pick up on a soldier. He was in a green dress uniform, standing at the table looking at a map. As I began to try and communicate with him, he changed. A bullet hole formed in his fore head and blood began to run down his face. Just then another investigator entered the room and asked me to go into the room on the other side to see if I felt anything. I had lost contact with the soldier, so I proceeded to walk to the other room.

As I turned the corner, I ran directly into it. It was tall, so tall that its head was tilted to be able to fit in the room. I reached slightly above navel height. Its white body glistened with a sort of wetness. Thin waist and barrel chested. Very long arms hands and fingers. No hair and no ears visible, webbed mouth and dark eyes. I could not tell gender. I broke out in a sweat, my heart pounding. I turned and walked away. The next part I do not remember, I was told by the other investigators. I guess that I walked out of the room very quickly very stiff mumbling "Too big, I do not like it" over and over. The next thing that I remember was being back in the original room that I was in. The other investigators had asked me what I had saw. Now normally when I experience something, I may tell one or two investigators to validate. I keep quiet to the rest as not to influence the investigation. For some reason this time, I had to say what happened. After a short while, we moved out of the room. Some of us split off and some went into the room directly under the room we were just in. As I stood there, I saw the White Entity slip through the ceiling from the room above. Then I could no longer see it. There was a closet type of room in the back of the bigger room that we were in. My brother said that he felt uneasy about the small space. As I looked in there, the White Entity was in there. It beckoned me into the closet, but I could not force myself to enter. I stood in the doorway asking what it wanted, but it would not answer me. After a few moments, I decided to enter. The second I did, it was gone.

I saw it one more time that night. I was sitting in the case mate running an E.V.P. session. Out of nowhere, a vision came into my head. The White Entity was coming down the outer case mate tunnel form the direction of the building we just left. This time it was different though. It was back lit with a bright light. It had multiple arms and heads as if it was entangled with multiple spirits. I snapped out of my thoughts and ran towards the tunnel, nothing was there.

The second sighting of the White Entity was seen at a case we were doing in Sterling Heights Michigan. Again, I believe it had nothing to do with the location. I believe it was there for me to see, but I do not know why. We were in the back bedroom where earlier, I was seeing a shadow of a man. It was myself and two other investigators including my brother. It seemed pretty normal at first. Then I had seen the White Entity coming down the hallway. It looked more similar to the way it looked in the case mate tunnel. As it reached the room, it disappeared. Now I did not say anything to the other investigators until later as not to influence them. At the point that it would have entered the room, one of the investigators said that the room felt different and it did. After a few moments, the White Entity raised up through the floor it was standing behind my brother. It was tilting its head and moving its webbed mouth, as to be talking or mocking. On a side note, my wife Darlene earlier that night, heard a chomping sound. Did it have anything to do with this, I do not know. I said, "What do you want what are you doing?" The other investigators had no idea what I was talking about. At that same instance, my brother said he felt uncomfortable and was going to step outside. Later on that evening I told him why. Shortly after that, the White Entity was gone again. I would also like to add, while speaking of this case, that in the same room that this took place earlier in the evening, I had seen a dark figure standing in the corner. The feeling that I got from it was a father figure. I did ask it if it was a father, but when reviewing the evidence, I did not receive an answer. So a feeling this will remain. However, the evidence that we did capture on this investigation was pretty interesting.

The next few encounters I had with the White Entity were brief. I had seen it in my home a few times, but they were very quick encounters. A few seconds at best. I had also seen it at my place of work. I had turned the corner to head down an aisle and there it was just standing there. A few seconds later, it was gone. At these times, it seemed like it was there just long enough for me to get that bizarre feeling

The next encounter was much briefer. We were doing a cemetery tour. At one point, I was picking up on a young child. I looked over to the wooded area for some reason and there it was standing in the brush. I handed the Spirit Box to person on the tour and said that I would be right back. I walked over to the area where I had seen the entity with recorder in hand. I did not see it, but began asking questions and hoping to finally get some answers. None were given.

We were on our second trip to the Trinway, Ohio location. The experiences at this location were so profound, that we had gone back a second time. I had unfinished business there, but we will get into those encounters in a bit. I and my wife Darlene were in the basement of the location. We had had some experiences down there, but we were on our way out. I stopped and turned, looking at the end of the long basement hall. Darlene asked me what was going on. At the very end of the hall, standing with the little girl and the angry woman (Two of the spirits of this location) was the White Entity. They stood there for a moment, turned and all walked away. For a time I thought that maybe this is where the White Entity was supposed to be or wanted to be. I thought it was going to be the last time that I was going to see it. I was wrong.

The last time that I have seen it, was the night that I had spoke of earlier. The night of the hospital dream and the mass amount of spirits in the hall. As I looked up at it from my bed,

I felt at ease for the first time with this being. It turned at walked to block to door, as to keep the hospital people out of my room. To enforce my rule of staying out of the rooms. I almost felt it to be as a guardian. Something to watch over me as I come in contact with the spirit world and travels into the afterlife. Can I be sure that this is the White Entities purpose? Of course not, but since then, where I have felt it, I have never seen it again, for now. On one last strange note, after I had painted the White Entity my daughter said "Didn't you draw that before?" She as right. I had did a picture about a year before called The Horde, but it pictured multiples of the White Entity. Is this something that I have known? Just did not remember? Was the times that it looked like it had the multiple heads and limbs just a bunch of them? These are questions that I am still trying to answer

July 14th 2014: I was speaking to someone today about the White Entity and as I was thinking back to the encounters with it, along with some other encounters. I began re-thinking about the Horde picture that I had done like a year prior to the first encounter. The person that I had been talking to me threw out the idea that perhaps it had been with me much longer than I had thought. Then something hit me. The picture from my home that I had caught way before even the team was thought of. The picture of the white face in the door wall looks very similar to the White Entity to me. This has only opened up more questions for me.

Sketch of the White Entity

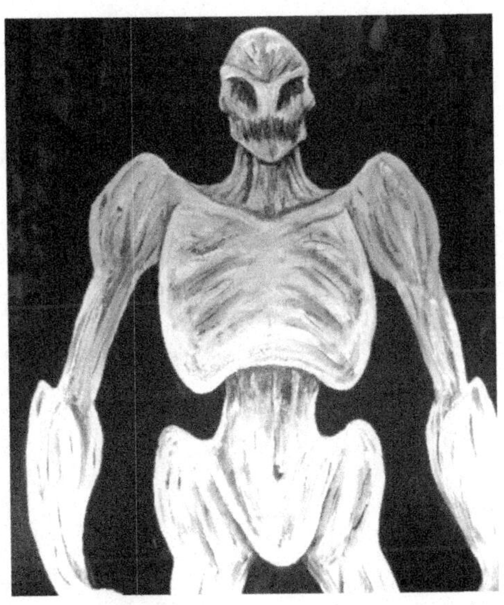

Sketch of the picture I did called "The Horde"

The First Opening

The first time I had opened myself fully, to have communication with the dead, was much unexpected. Yes, I know I had asked for it and it was already happening to a point. I thought instead of bits and pieces it may be nice to get the whole story. I just did not expect it to be so fast or accurate.

We were on a case in Armada Michigan. This was a brother of one of the investigators house. The family had no ties to this house or property. The home was just old and they asked if we would come out to investigate it. We went in treating it more like an interview. We would ask about the happenings and do small sessions to see if we would pick up on anything.

After a few sessions throughout the house, we were sitting in the living room. I was on the couch. Suddenly, I could see a thin woman in a white dress standing at the top of the stairs. Now, I could not actually see the stairs, just the image. The woman had disheveled brown hair and a black spot on her throat. I just assumed it was a broach or something. I asked my wife to started taking pictures towards the stair area. Now I did not mention any of this, in fear I may be out of my mind. She took the pictures and we ended our session headed down to the basement and did another.

When we came back up from the basement, I could not shake that feeling. Me and my brother proceeded to the stairs to start a new E.V.P. session. I was sitting on the stairs and he was standing above me in the small hall at the top of the stairs. We were asking your standard questions - name, age, that kind of stuff. My questioning then suddenly changes to questions of murder and choking. The reason for the question changes? I was no longer seeing my brother. Although he was still standing there, I was seeing the woman holding her throat. At the time I did not understand what she was trying to tell me, but I soon would.

We finished up and were packing up the equipment. The others knew something was wrong with me, but I kept saying that nothing was wrong. I did not know how to handle what was happening to me that night.

On the drive home, Darlene finally got it out of me. I explained to her what had happened.

The next day, myself and my brother were heading to do a side job. I thought he should know as well, so I also gave him the details of what had happened the night before. It is a good thing that I had told somebody what was going on. It would help to validate later on what I had seen.

A few days later I was reviewing evidence. I came across an E.V.P. that said "I'm Michaels Aunt." It was in a soft whispery voice. Now to understand better, me and my brother did not grow up together. At this point, we had only been together for a short time and most of it was to do with the team and the paranormal. So I did not know any of his life or his wife's. Being as this was my brother's wife's brother's house, I hope everyone caught that, I shot her a text. I asked her "Did you guys have an aunt that died?" She text me back "How did you know that?" I told her that I had just caught an E.V.P. that had told me so. She called me right away. The first thing that I had asked her was did her aunt have short brown hair. She told me that they had cut it short when they put the trach in. I basically dropped my phone. In that instant, I knew what the black spot on her throat was, it was not a broach, it was where they did the tachometry. I then asked her if she would tell me how she died. She told me she died of throat cancer. Again, I was floored. That is why she was holding her throat on the stairs. Finally, she had told me that her aunt was buried in a white dress.

Of course she had told her family. They all had mixed emotions. Understandably so. The mother, however, wanted to hear the E.V.P.'s. We all went down to my brothers basement and hooked up the digital recorder to the big speakers. We played the E.V.P. for her, but I am not sure how she felt about it. We had another E.V.P. Though, from the same investigation and in the same voice. It said, “I’m not ready yet."

Now we did not think into this one too much. When the mother heard it, she ran upstairs crying. After she composed herself she came back downstairs. She then proceeded to tell us that her sister said that to her every day before she died.

Now this is where I get my theory that the spirit world knows what is going on and who is willing to help get their messages across. The house had nothing to do with the family or the aunt. The messages were, I believe for the aunt’s sister, not the people living in the house. I strongly believe that the aunt knew that we were going to be at that house, that we would be trying to capture evidence and that I was opened to the communication. That the messages would get back to her sister. They did. I do not know why or exactly what they were meant for, but they did.

Sketch of the woman that I saw on the landing

The Second Encounter

Prospect Place: Trinway, Ohio

Brief History: Prospect Place is also known as Trinway Mansion and Prospect Place Mansion. It is a 29-room mansion built by George Willison Adams in Trinway, Ohio. It is just north of Dresden and was built in 1856. Today it is the home of the non-profit G. W. Adams Educational Center, Inc. The mansion is also listed on the National Register of Historic Places and the Ohio Underground Railroad Association's list of Underground Railroad sites.

Haunted History

These are the stories that have been told and should not be considered as historically documented.

There is a tale of a bounty hunter that had visited Prospect Place from the south and demanded that all slaves in hiding there be turned over. George Adams the owner of the property proceeded to produce from his coat a Navy revolver and a stand-off with the heavily armed Bounty hunter took place for several minutes. Seeing the predicament, the ranch hands working in the barn at the time quickly emerged with their rifles. The Bounty Hunter deciding that the situation had become too dangerous, retreated to his camp empty handed of any slaves. It is then said that the ranch hands decided to take on a little vigilante justice in their own hands, unknown to George. They tracked the bounty hunter to his camp, kidnapped him and took him back to the barn located on the property. There they had a trial and hung him in the barn, burying the body in an unknown location. It is now said that the spirit of the bounty hunter haunts the barn looking for revenge on those who hung him.

A young girl afflicted with a fever wandered onto the balcony one cold night in the winter, lost her footing and fell over the low railing to the hard sandstone steps below. The girl's body was not buried immediately as the ground was frozen and would not allow for the digging of a grave. Her body was placed on ice in the basement in a pit originally designed as a refrigeration system for the home. Here the child remained. When the spring thaw would arrive, she could be given a proper burial. The mother grieving for her lost child, visited the body every day until the burial. Today it is said that ghost of the little girl can sometimes be seen on the second floor by the door that was once was the entrance to the balcony. Others have seen her in the basement, the ballroom and the Upstairs Parlor which is today the guest bedroom. The first time that I had seen her personally was in the basement.

Anna is another spirit who is said to be here along with her husband William. William had strangely disappeared on a trip to take care of some personal business and Anna died in Prospect Place due to complications from a fall on the ice at the neighboring River Dale mansion. She died lonely and broken, never knowing the fate of her missing husband. It is said that Anna still wanders the halls of Prospect Place searching for the life and husband she once loved. The first time that I was here I caught an E.V.P. of a man calling her name. I also believe that this may be the woman that I encountered.

It is also said that there is a spirit of a refugee woman that had died and is in the basement. It is also said that she is known to play pranks from time to time. There is also said to be a spirit of a servant seen on the stairwell between the second floor and the ballroom.

For more information please visit: www.gwacenter.org

These entities that I encountered at the place in Trinway Ohio affected me so intensely, that we went back within a few months. I could not let it go. I had to get back and finish something. I just was not sure what.

The first spirit that I had encountered was on the first day, shortly after we had arrived. On the first day there were only four of us, myself my brother and our two wives.

I and my brother were setting up the DVR cameras while our wives were getting the grill going. I had headed down to the basement to set the camera while my brother was hooking the wires to the system. Now as the story goes, a young child sick with fever resting on the second floor awoke looking for her mother and fell to her death off of the second floor balcony. With the ground being frozen and too hard to dig a grave, they kept the young girl's body in the basement in the well system were it would stay cool. The mother would go and visit for hours with her deceased daughter's body in the basement until the day came when the ground was soft enough to bury her.

As I was setting the camera, I was not even facing the door that contains the well, but even with my back to it, I could see the young girl standing there. She stood about three to three and a half feet tall, her hands behind her back as she rocked back and forth from heel to toe. As if wondering what I was doing. She was barefooted and only wore what looked like a nightgown of sorts. Being fairly new to the opening of communication that I had done, I was more than slightly uncomfortable and wanted to leave the basement. Not from the child herself, but from the unexpectedness of the situation. I left the basement and told what had happened to me to the other three investigators that were there. After I was able to collect my thoughts, I had returned to the basement to set up the IR lights for the DVR camera. She did not reveal herself again until later.

I am now going to skip around the events of the investigation so that all of the experiences of the child are all together. Later that evening, as we were investigating the well room, the young child kept running up and down the hall and peeking in the door as if to be playing a game with us. Again, I did not see her physically. I could just see her. After about three trips up and down the basement hall, I could not see her anymore. Also understand that, in this basement there is an overwhelming sadness that I still cannot shake to this day.

While investigating on the second floor of the first night, I was hit with a sadness that I could not stop. To the point that there were tears in my eyes. Just as that was happening, one of the investigators was sure that she had seen the child standing on the stairs, but it was just for a split second that she had seen her.

On the second day, we had traveled to the cemetery to find the family graves of the residence that had lived at this location. We had found this grave who I believe may belong to the child in the basement.

Shortly after, the team had arrived and after we had given them a tour of the grounds I was standing by the basement window and once again saw the child with her face and hands pressed up against the window. Now the window is about five feet off the basement ground. Another investigator had seen me doing something by the window and had come over to see what was going on. We had started taking pictures, but she was gone.

Later that night, we had all split up into smaller groups and spread throughout the basement. Right at the beginning of the session, the sadness was apparent. Only to be cut short by the female entity that I will speak of next. It was as if she had grabbed the girl away, I kept hearing "I told you not to speak to them, this was the plan" and the basement felt empty. Even with the eight investigators spread about.

The last encounter that I had with the child is a little more personal to me. We had just finished packing up the van and the team had just left. I was sitting in the side of the van facing the basement window. There she was, waving good bye to me. I waved back, but I cannot even begin to explain the sadness that I felt. It was as if I was leaving a child to an eternity trapped in a basement. Again, even as I write this now the sadness consumes me.

On the second trip back, the place felt less consuming. In fact, the only time that I saw the little girl was in the basement with the angry woman and the White entity. As I spoke about before.

Although the anger that I felt off this entity was quite real, do not mistake my feelings in the matter. I believe she had every right to be. Although we meant no harm and are only searching for answers in the realm of the paranormal, we and people like us, are the ones invading their space and their home. When it is a constant occurrence, well I know that at some point, I would be angry as well. In fact, this spirit, in a way, has changed the way that I will handle my investigations and the spirits that I encounter. I will no longer demand them to speak into the red light or show themselves to me on command and to just not to be so demanding of them. To show more respect. These are just my personal opinions and are not meant to offend any others in how they investigate.

Even on the tour during the first day, we all had felt something in the attic area.

Now I am not sure if this spirit is the one who caused this, but I feel that she is the strongest in the house. Like she runs the show and it is quite possibly her who did this. On the first night, the four of us began our investigation in the Ballroom located in the attic. Less than five minutes in, I lost it. My sight was going and I became very dizzy. I fell to one knee, back up and it hit me again. Down. I managed to make it to the chair that I was heading for in the first place. I was able to gather myself and continue with the investigation. Only a short time later, it hit me again just not as bad. In fact, during that same session, my brother had started to feel sick to his stomach. We had all felt drained for the rest of the night. I have never felt this loss of energy in any investigation. As well as the rest of us.

The second night became even more intense.

I and my wife Darlene were on the first floor gathering equipment from the front parlor, when Darlene noticed fellow investigator at the base of the stairs that head to the second floor. Something was going on. Within twenty seconds of being there, it hit me. Extreme anger and frustration. My whole body began to tingle as it in the attic, several times the day before. Even Darlene and the investigator had felt the same. I do not know if it was as intense as my own, but that is their story to tell.

Suddenly, there she was at the top of the stairs, pacing back and forth shaking her head, as I found myself doing the same.

Yet I kept saying, "No No No No!" Darlene and the investigator kept seeing the spots from the laser grid disappear and then reappear. I did not. All I could see was her. In fact, there were things said by the two ladies that I did not even recall. I had only heard their conversation on listening back the digital recorder.

The spirit was angry with us and the continuing situation in her home. All I kept hearing was "Why are they constantly here. I am tired of performing. No more, sick of it!" and then I got such a feeling of anger. Like she was about to shoot down to stairs and do something drastic. I grabbed Darlene by the arm and said, "Move, get out of the way!" As I pulled her away from the base of the stairs with a definite urgency, all three of us felt this and decided to exit the building.

Even as we stood outside trying to collect ourselves, I could feel her watching us from the second floor window. We all could, but she was not alone. There were two small boys with her. One in each of the other windows. They were hard to see and said nothing. They all just watched. I do not know anything about the two boys and that was the only time that I had seen them. The feeling was so intense, that not a one of us wanted to look up. Darlene with her back to the building did not even want to turn around. I did look up though. Nothing physically was there and after a short while the feelings had left.

At this point we all felt comfortable enough to go back in. We headed to home base where we had explained to the rest of the team what had happened. The team being the team headed straight up to the second floor to investigate, as that is what we were there for. My sister-in-law had stayed behind with the three of us. I could hear the investigation going on upstairs. As I looked up from the DVR monitor, I could see her. The body tingling came back and there she was standing in the doorway of home base. She was angrier now than before. I think at me personally. All I kept hearing was "I thought that I had told you, why you let them go up there." She as yelling at me. Just then, and maybe I shouldn't have said anything, I stated that she was there and watching us. My sister-in-law grabbed my arm and could not hold her grip. She later told us that when she grabbed me, it was like I had just gotten out of a swimming pool. I was soaked and her hand slipped right off. Darlene would not turn to the door and the other investigator, I think felt angry in her own right. She rushed to the door and slammed it exclaiming "You cannot come in here!"

Now I understand what she was doing and how she felt that she had to deal with it. I have done it in my own home, restricting where the spirits may go, but like I said before, this is her home we were the invaders in her space. Although I am kind of glad that she did, the spirit retreated to the front parlor, or so I felt and the feelings in the room had subsided. Let me add again, these are my personal feelings on the matter. I would never want to offend anyone on how they would treat a situation. We must all do what we feel is right for us and to keep ourselves and our team safe. These were just the feelings that I was getting and understanding from the female entity. Feelings so strong in fact, that this spirit and what she had been communicating to me is my reason for changing the way that I will handle future investigations.

We all met back up and decided to give the house a break. The team headed out to the barn to investigate, where at this time my brother was going to have his own personal experience, which we will be told of at a later time.

After my brother's experience and after grounding myself, the team headed back in. We all spread out through the first floor, still within the proximity of the staircase. I had started seeing physical shadows moving about from the landing to the first floor. Not on the stair case, but on the side of it. Shortly after, an investigator felt as if the woman was crying, that she could not get us to leave. I too saw her crouched down in the landing doorway, but I could not see her face. Then it had got more bizarre. I could see her coming through the floor, behind us at the same time. Almost as if to check our reactions of what was going on. She did this several times before I could finally see her face from her crouched position. The first words out of my mouth were “False she is being false.” She was laughing at us, that we had believed, that she was in despair for not getting us to leave. As soon as I had said this, she became angered again pacing on the second floor "What to do next, thinking...thinking." My hand had begun shaking and I did not even realize it. After a few moments, it was as if she had retreated to the back of the house to regroup herself. We placed a digital recorder and a REM Pod at the top of the stairs, a REM Pod will light up and make a buzzing noise if anything breaks the field around it. Most of the team had went outside to investigate. I and an investigator were monitoring the DVR system, debunking the flashlights coming through the second floor windows and Darlene and my sister-in-law were headed to the restroom. The buzzing began the REM Pod at the top of the stairs was going off. At first I did not realize what I was hearing, but as soon as I did, we ran to the stairs at the same time. Darlene and my sister-in-law were also headed towards the stairs, but as soon as we turned the corner, the noise had stopped. We had seen no bats or anything at the surrounding area. I walkied the team and they came back in. With no further experiences going on, we decided to investigate the basement. This is where I feel that the female spirit who I felt was the strongest in the house, ran it if you will, shut down all of the activity in the house. As if not allowing anyone in the house to communicate with any of us. Again the house felt empty. There were e few more experiences that had happened outside the house later on, but the spirits of the house were done. I believe after the scaring or the feeling bad for her did not work, this was her alternative to make us leave and leave them alone. Now some who read this may very well just think that I am crazy or just making it up and that is fine, that is their choice. I was there and I know what had happened to me and again, that is all that matters. These experiences that I had at the location in Trinway, Ohio were profound enough to me that it has changed me as a person and a paranormal investigator. I feel that it has raised me and our team to the next level. I only hope that by writing my experience down, that I can finally get them out of my head. It has been a while now and I still cannot shake the feelings and spirits of that place.

Sketch of the Girl In The Basement

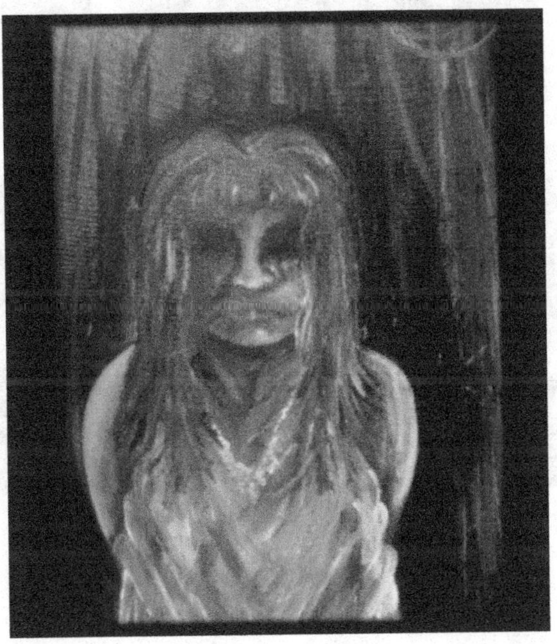

Sketch of the Angry Woman on the stairs

Actual Photo: This picture was caught in the basement by Darlene. The REM pod kept going off during this activity. It also, to me, does not look like any bug or dust that I have seen, but it is for you to decide.

Actual Photo: This was two different pictures. I combined them to easily show the comparison. Notice the black shadow figure in the window. Also notice how in the second picture that it moves to the other side of the window. Also, whatever it is, is pushing the shade back. The really cool thing about this is, we were standing outside and I had said that I felt like something was watching us from the building. An investigator, who was In **Into The AfterLife Paranormal** *at the time of this investigation, started snapping pictures shortly after and this is what was caught.*

Cemeteries

Let me start off by saying, although I do find cemeteries very interesting, I do not really like to investigate them. There is a lot of contamination from being outside. I also believe that if I was a spirit, I may visit my grave from time to time, but I would not hang out there. I would want to be around a place or person that had meant something to me. That being said, I have had some great experiences in them and have caught some compelling evidence. This first set of pictures comes from a cemetery that I use to pass on my way to my tattoo artist up in Attica Michigan. I had passed this cemetery several times before entering it. Something kept calling me into this location, so I decided to start bringing my camera with me when I was going for a tattoo session. These are the actual photos from this particular cemetery.

Actual Photo: This, To Me, Looks Like A Partial Face Manifesting. There Was Nothing Hanging In The Bush. It Is Very Similar To Something That I Had Caught In Mansfield.

Actual Photo: This Picture May Be A Little Harder To See. To Me It Looks As If There Is A Man With His Head Down. Possibly Wearing A Cap. Or Is This Just A Great Example Of Matrixing.

The Tour

We were invited first to do a meet and greet at a local shop located in Wood Haven Michigan at the Smokey Crystal Designs. From that, we were then invited to help host a tour in a local cemetery. It was actually a larger group. If I remember, it was about 25 people. It rained the full night and was pretty cold, but everyone had a great time. We had me and three other Into The AfterLife Paranormal investigators that night. We split into groups and ran 45 minute sessions. We would then move to next area. We had it mapped out to have each group be able to investigate the four corners of the cemetery. We had handed out some of our equipment and after explaining how it had worked, we let the people investigate with them. I personally had got the feeling of a small child following us around the whole time. I did pull away one of the people, who can also sense the dead, someone that I trust and she had said that she had sensed a small child as wel,l but was not clear if it was male or female. I also saw the White Entity in the bushes. I approached it and asked what it had wanted, but it turned and left. This was a great experience for me and the attending members of the team. It was our first tour and we had learned a lot.

This Picture Was Taken By An Into The AfterLife Investigator. It Was Taken The Night Of the Tour In The Bushes Were I Saw The White Entity. It Was Taken After My Group Had Left The Area And Theirs Moved In. I Am Not Saying That This Is A Ghost, Just A Weird Light That We Could Not Explain.

The Ohio State Reformatory: Mansfield Ohio

The Ohio State Reformatory is also known as the Mansfield Reformatory. It is a historic prison located in Mansfield, Ohio. It was built between 1886 and 1910 and remained in operation until a 1990 federal court ruling ordered the facility to be closed. This facility has used in a number of films TV shows and music videos. The Reformatory doors were opened to its first 150 young offenders in September 1896. After housing over 155,000 men in its lifetime the doors to the prison closed December 31, 1990. To this day the Ohio State Reformatory Historic Site receives visitors from all over the world. Every year tourist's, movie buffs and paranormal investigators walk through the halls of this majestic and historical structure.

Haunted History

There are many stories and documented paranormal experiences from this location. Many have been pushed, felt the chills of a presence, heard voices and cell doors slamming and have seen dark apparitions. There are tales of the spirit of the guard that was killed in solitary confinement, as well as the inmate that was hung in the shower room. Also, tales of the Wardens wife wandering the halls who accidentally shot herself in the Wardens Mansion. There are too many stories to write about here. That would probably take a whole other book, but this is just a sample of some of the things that you could expect while visiting there.

For More Information Please Visit: www.mrps.org.

This was the first location that I officially investigated. I overheard a co-worker named Keri, who later became a member of the team and a very good friend, talking about this place. I saw the pictures that she had taken. I was intrigued, but I never said anything. I transferred from that location. Six months later, I transferred back. This time when I heard her talking about it again, I asked if I could see the pictures. The location looked fantastic. She filled me in about the public investigations. We booked it right away.

The first time at this location, well it is hard to describe. I was in awe when we pulled up and I could not wait to enter. It was also the beginning of mine and Darlene's paranormal adventures.

I will say though, as excited as I was, I was still apprehensive about such things as doing EVP sessions. To be truthful, I felt kind of stupid talking to no one. Man I was never more wrong. If I had known then what I know now, it would have been totally different. I think that's why I have gone back so many times. The evidence that I have caught there is unbelievable. Although I did capture some good evidence the first time, and it was an awesome experience, I was just starting. As I look back now, I wish I would have put more into it. I did get my chance though.

The first was a public event. The second we booked a private investigation. Fifteen people. What a night. Although I had not opened myself up at this point, there was still a lot of interaction with the afterlife. Rocks thrown and confirmed on digital recorder a male voice saying, “Did throw a rock."

Let’s start with the first investigation though. I and Darlene were very excited to be there. Although, I think that I may have been a tad bit more excited I kept taking off from the group all night.

When we first pulled up, I was in awe and I could not believe on what we were about to do. I had waited my whole life for something like this.

My first really good paranormal photo was caught at this location. It was on the tour of the place. I was taking random shots. It appears to be a woman standing in the doorway, her hands on the shoulders of a boy. They were both standing in a doorway in one of the staff housing areas. When it was a functional facility. It was as if they were watching the people on the tour.

Later that evening, as we walked by the cells Darlene began to choke out of nowhere. Is this paranormal or could it just be coincidence. I do not know for sure. As we made it to the upper cells, I heard what sounded like feet scuffling right in front of me. I ran down to the end of the cells to see if any other investigators were around. No one was to be found. Now I do have to admit, this first time out I felt kind of stupid doing E.V.P. sessions. I did not really speak and there was a lot of movement noises contaminating the sessions. Man did I regret that. If I knew then what I know now, it would have been a totally different experience, but I guess you have to start somewhere. I also caught what seemed to be a boy in the basement and a face in a shower room. In fact, these pictures that I caught at this location are the best that I ever have. I did not know what was captured at the time and I did not care. The experience in itself was enough for me, the pictures were a bonus.

May 19th 2011: So we missed a summer of going back to this location. Although I did still investigate other locations that summer, and it made me want to go back. I felt like I had jipped myself by being timid the year before. So the next summer we booked a private investigation. Fifteen people. Many of who would later become some of the first members of Into The AfterLife Paranormal.

We arrive once again, and once again the sight of this location did not disappoint. In fact, I think that we were all in awe. Once inside before, we split into smaller groups, we all went to do a session in the sub-basement under solitary confinement. The session went well. No feelings though, at least from myself and no one else had said anything. So we left split into our smaller groups to cover more area. There were only the fifteen of us, as opposed to the hundred in the public tour two years prior. We had a lot of ground to cover.

I and my wife Darlene went into solitary confinement. Right away, I was having problems with the equipment. The camera would not stay on. Now we did have a digital recorder sitting in the ramped doorway just outside of the cell that we were sitting in. She them proceeds to call out to the entities that may have been in the area. We caught an awesome E.V.P. It said "I will kill him" and them a fainter second voice "Why do you need to kill him". Now when I first heard of this, I thought why do they want to kill me!!! After a while and a little more of a calm head, I now feel that it was residual. There is a story of a guard getting killed by an inmate in the shower room at the end of the hall. I now assume that it was the prisoner that committed the tragic act plotting it out. I am not even going to say that it was an entity of the prisoners, but possibly an imprint left in the area. This was a very tragic event and must have left some kind of bad energy imprinted in this area. We also caught an E.V.P. that said "Let me out" and we had a great Spirit Box session as well. After that session, we proceeded to the second floor of solitary. We later found after reviewing 8mm camera footage, that as we were walking up the stairs to the second floor, we caught this strange mist coming out of the wall. On the second floor we set up a flashlight on a chair and proceeded to ask questions. Very soon after we started to get direct responses to our yes and no questions. Once again not known to us at the time, in the background of the 8mm footage, a strange light manifested hung for a few moments and slowly faded away. There was nobody else in the area or even close. Happy with the flashlight session we packed up and decided t move locations.

Me and Darlene wandered around for a bit doing small sessions throughout different locations in the prison. We finally came across three of the investigators sitting in the hall outside some of the cells. They did not seem to be having very many experiences. We asked them if they would like to join us in the shower room that was down the hall. Now this is a different shower room than the one just spoke. We entered the shower room and began to set up our equipment. I had ask to myself where should I put the recorder I got a response, "Where you want" We then caught the same voice saying "Leave me alone." Again, at the time we did not know this. We started to get flashlight responses once again and a final E.V.P in this location a wicked laugh.

We then ended up in the hospital area. It was myself, Darlene and three other investigators. We had begun our session running the usual equipment. Being in the hospital area we wanted to keep the questions in theme of the area. Darlene then began to ask how they had passed. She got the answer of "Throat Cancer." We had caught more E.V.P.'s in this area as well, but what happened next was incredible. A bunch of small rocks were thrown at us. It was as if someone scooped up a handful of pebbles and chucked them at us. You could hear them all scatter across the floor. We were all in shock. I then started up the Spirit Box and began to ask questions. Among then I had asked if someone had thrown the rocks at us. My response was "Did throw a rock." Now this too was incredible, especially for a Spirit Box answer. First off, to be able to get a full sentence is hard enough, but to get one that is a direct response to your question, is even better.

Another place that we had good responses was in one of the Mansions that are connected to the prison. We all had joined back up to do a mass group session. We all sat about the area running our equipment. We caught a name on the Spirit Box. One that ties into the location that we were at.

We continued investigating by ourselves, the group had went their own ways again. It was getting to the end of the night. Myself and Darlene were walking on the bottom floor by the cells, and once again on the 8mm camera, a misty figure was caught. It was as if to move out of Darlene's way. It was much bigger than the mist on the stairs and this time I had seen it in the camera screen while I was filming. Very excited, I reviewed the footage right then and there. Sure enough, there it was. I showed Darlene and we both were in awe.

We met up in another shower room with most of the other investigators. This would end up to be our last session for that night. We ran the equipment as we had been doing, but while the feeling that had been there the whole night was still there, nothing really happened.

I must say that this private tour that we did that night was one of my most awesome experiences. This location has become one of my favorite locations to investigate. So much so that I have been back two more times to date.

The location hosts a volunteer program were you help clean up and work. Then later that night you get to investigate for free. To me, this is a great trade-off. You get to take part in helping restore a historical location. To clean and maintain it, and believe me you do work. The bonus is, a free investigation of one of the most haunted places that I have been. For many paranormal investigators this is a great deal. We all know that this is not a field to get into for financial gain so anything like this is great for us.

Unfortunately, for the first clean-up my wife Darlene could not attend. A few members of the team went with me. We arrived on a Saturday morning. Our detail was to clean the basement and believe me when you are there to work, you work. We were ahead of schedule and the basement was cleared out before lunch. We then moved into the mansions to haul out these metal gates. Soon our work day was done we enjoyed dinner and some of us rested. Not me, I become far too excited on investigations to sleep or even rest. It was now time to investigate. It was a very cold night, but that was not going to stop me. We started in Solitary Confinement. A short time in, I began to see three men standing down at the far end. One who I assume was the leader, was huge. The two others were much smaller. We were running recorders and I was trying to communicate with them. It seemed like they were just content with watching what we were doing. After a while they took off, me and another investigator followed. We headed in the direction that they did but I could no longer pick up on them.

We continued to investigate through the night. We lost some investigators to the cold and to sleep. We did however, catch an odd video from one of the cells. It appears to be some kind of weird shadow type thing crouching down as the investigators camera turned into the cell. We finished off the night in one of the rooms in one of the staffs quarters. It had heat. I lasted until about 4am. Even though I went to bed, I did not sleep. It was far too cold, but still worth the experience.

The second time out to the clean-up was much better. Mostly for the reason that Darlene was able to go this year. Another plus was that we went down with some of our good friends Mike and Stephanie. They are investigators with another Michigan team. In fact, we have become friends with the whole team and have learned a lot from them.

This time we arrived the Friday night before. We set up in a much warmer place. We were able to hang out with some great and friendly people. The volunteers that run the haunted events and help take care of the facility. We did go out that night and walk around. Some of the crew took us to places that we have never been. At one point, we ended up in the basement. This is where I saw the prisoner looking entity standing at the top of the staircase. Although I did do a sketch later that night and showed Darlene, I did not mention it to anyone else. We kept getting told to have fun trying to sleep in the room that we were in. It was a room with an electric chair on display. It was probably one of the better nights that I have slept in a while.

We awoke and prepared to start to work. We were lucky enough to work in a room that would soon become the administrative room. I tore up an old floor in the kitchen area that was discovered behind a sealed off wall. Darlene and Stephanie prepped the walls for primer and paint. There were also two others that were there helping, one being our supervisor. We finished the room. To be honest, I did not think that we would. The paint went up much faster than I thought.

After dinner we hung out with the group again, but soon me and my wife went out to investigate. It was like it was supposed to be, me and her together investigating a team of two. These are my favorite times while investigating. We went from place to place. Eventually we went back and brought some of the group with us once. In the chapel area we caught an odd name on the Spirit Box that coincided with one of the nicknames of a volunteer. We went down to show her. We then, with her and our friend Stephanie, headed back up to the chapel to do a session. We did pick up on some more strange Spirit Box answers. We all went back to the main area. After another time out, me and Darlene went back to hang with the group. Darlene had fallen down the stairs that night in the cells. She jacked up her ankle. That morning however, I felt that I did not go to every location that I wanted to that I had shorted myself. So while everyone still slept, Darlene and myself went to all of the places that we missed from the night before and we ran short sessions. While we were walking along the one of the cell wing,s we both heard one of the cell doors bang or move directly behind us. It was very loud and we saw no one around. Although it seemed almost peaceful in there, there was a strange howl from the wind rushing through the corridor. It sounded like multiple banshee screams. At one point we thought we heard what sounded like a human whistle amongst the wind. With the wind being so strong through the area though, I feel that I must chalk it up to exactly that, the wind. Although the basement entity was the only thing that I saw that trip, I had a great time investigating. We met a lot of new and great people. Hung out with old friends and new and I feel that me and Darlene were able to have a great connection investigating together.

When I first captured these pictures, I had emailed them right away to the reformatory. I do not know if they had ever seen them, but would be very interested on their thoughts. With them being there all of the time, I am sure that they would have some great insights or theories.

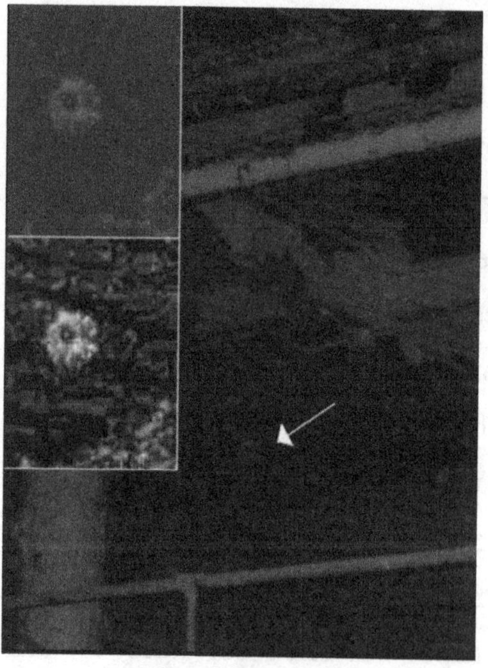

This Is What I Call "The Face" It Was A Random Picture That I Took While Investigating This Location. It Is In The Corner Of the Shower Room Up Towards The Ceiling.

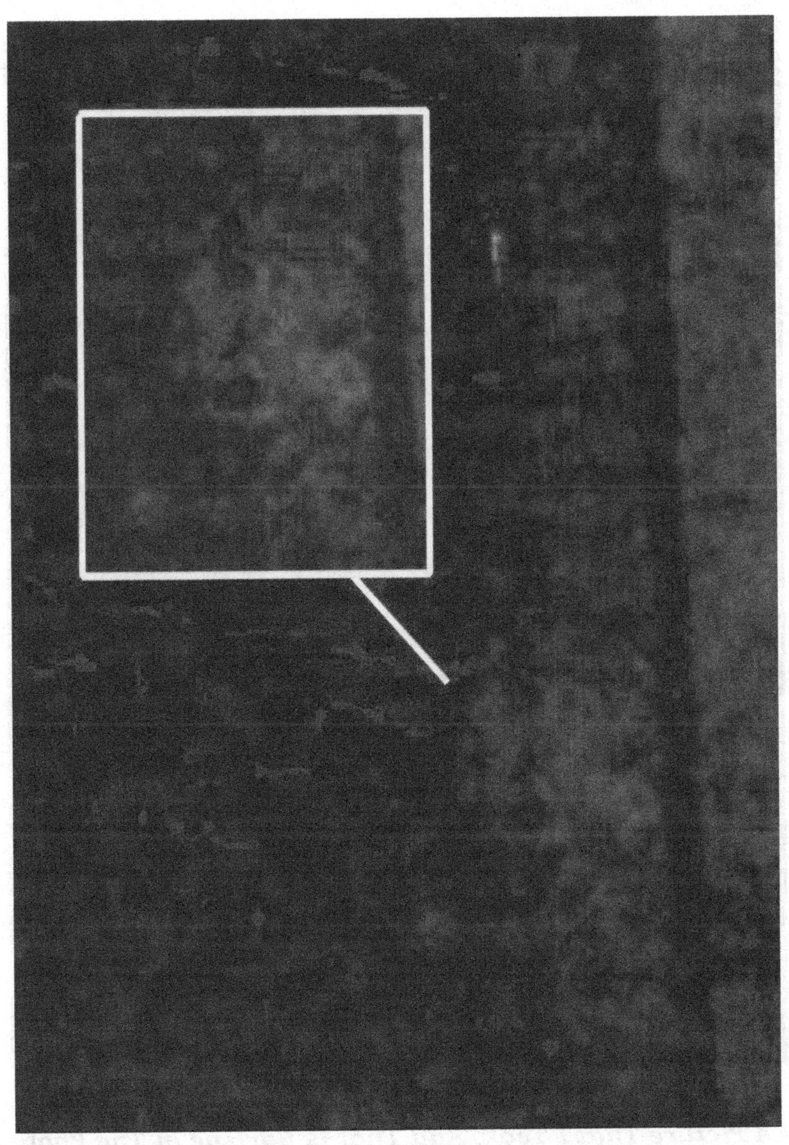

This Is A Weird Face-Like Image That I Caught On Camera. To Me, I Have Never Seen Dust That Had This Sort Of Shape To It. Along with Pretty Distinct Facial Features.

This Is A Picture That I Took, And That Is Darlene In The Photo. Now I Am Really Not An "Orb" Person And I Know That 99 Percent Of the Time It Is Dust Or A Bug, Or Even Something Random Such As A Hair, But This Anomaly Looks To Be Omitting Its Own Light. It Also Looks To Be Reflecting Off The Window In The Back Of the Room. Am I Saying It Is A Ghost? No, Just Strange.

Actual Photo: This Photo Was Taken By Myself In The Basement. This Is A Lighter Version Of the Original Picture. You Can See What Appears To Be Someone Sitting On The Floor. It Looks As If It Is Looking Back At Me. You Can See The Face And A Fisted Hand Towards The Bottom Of the Picture

Actual Photo: First Picture I Took Of What Appears To Be Two Apparitions

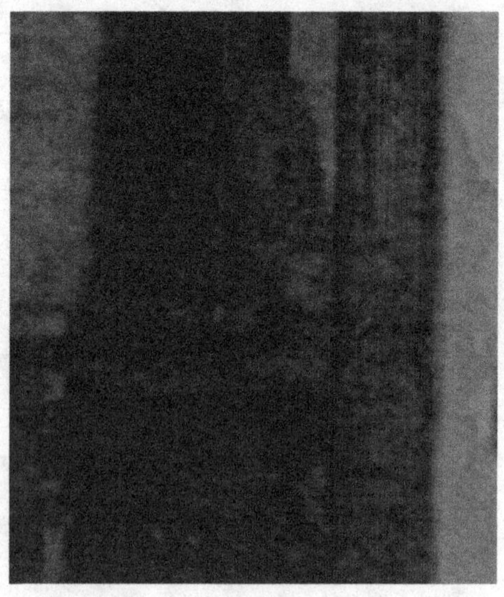

Same Picture As Above, Closer And Lightened Up. I See What Appears To Be A Female And A Younger Person Standing In Front Of Her. They Appear To Be Watching Again. This Was Taken Randomly And During The Day

Sketch Of the Entity I Saw At The Top Of the Basement Stairs On The Night Before The Clean-Up

[illegible]

Scots On The Night Before The Clean-Up

Metamora Michigan

March 29th 2013: We picked up a case in Metamora Michigan. It was on an old farmhouse that was built in 1900 and sits on 28 acres of farmland. There are stories of a family burial plot on the land, some of the claims include movement of objects, voices, noises and shadow people. There was also the claim of a strange green light that had shot up from the kitchen floor.

When we arrived, the team went on the tour of the house. I stayed back to start setting up the equipment. It was also so that I would not hear the stories or descriptions of the entities believed to be in the home. I did not want to be influenced in case of maybe seeing something.

The first entity that I encountered came from the surrounding land. We were out in the woods between a stream and an old hunter's homemade shelter. I was running my Spirit Box. After a while, a female voice came through and said "Hi." Nothing more was heard during this session. As we were walking the path in the woods that led back to the house, I was heading up the group and then I saw her. It was for but a brief moment, but she was there. A pale woman in a white dress and dark hair. Her white dress was flowing in the night air as if in a movie. As fast as she was there, she was gone. I told the team members that were there and we proceeded back to the client's house.

Later that night, myself and my brother went to the second floor to begin a session. The rest of the investigators were still on the first floor. He was running his camera and I began an E.V.P. session on my digital recorder. It was then that I had begun to pick up a boy in the closet of the clients son. He was a bigger boy, somewhat tall and chubby. I think he was between the ages of ten to twelve, but he had the mental state of someone much younger. Another few features that stood out were a long crew cut and a striped shirt. He would not come out of the closet. It was like it was his safe haven. I later learned from the client that there was a story of an abusive mother and that she had locked her kids in the closet among other things. My theory on that is, if we were forced to stay in the closet all of the time that is where he would feel the safest in life and in death. Now here is an even stranger part. We had been out to the clients several times. We ended up having some tours of the house with other paranormal investigators. One of these people ended up joining Into The AfterLife Paranormal. She was reviewing her files from a more recent case that we had done. On the disc was the photos from the Metamora tour. She posted a pick taken from the outside of the home. In the window of one of the bedrooms, is what appears to be a boy sitting there in a striped shirt. She posted it on our private team page. The homeowner, who also ended up becoming a team member, said that she has a sketch that I did for her of the boy. No one up until then had seen this sketch. It was then shared with the rest of the team. It sent shivers through our bodies as we compared the two.

Original Sketch Of the Boy In The Closet

In the same session, after the encounter with the boy, I then saw a very tall man standing in the doorway of the room. He was wearing a white button up shirt, suspenders and a tweed type pant. His hair was brown and curly slightly receding. An older man, possibly between Forty and Fifty. He looked like he may have been from an earlier era. I began to describe him to my brother on camera. After the session, we proceed to head downstairs. I need to now ask the client the description of the known entities in the home. She then proceeds to describe the exact man to me that I had just seen. Later on, I end up sketching the man and giving it to her. She also gives me a bit of believed background on the male spirit. He was believed to be a cross dresser and had woman's clothing hid in there attic. Now this information comes from a Shaman that they had out prior to us, so take it as you will. It did get me thinking though, and we discussed this theory amongst a few of the team members. What if the tall man and the boy were the same entity? His younger self hidden away, possibly ashamed, because let's face it, back in an earlier time people did not except anything that would be considered different. He would probably have to have kept it hidden. I actually, at a later investigation, tried to explain to the entity that if this was true, there is no longer a need to hide it. That those times had changed and that it was much more accepted in today's society and that no one should have to hide who they truly are. Did it help him I do not or may not ever know? I can only hope that if this is the case maybe it gave him some peace.

Original Sketch Of the Tall Man

I had one more encounter with the tall man at this location. We were on another investigation at this location. We were doing a session in the back bedroom. I then saw him peering in through the windows. He was moving back and forth between the two windowed sides of the room. It was almost instantly from window to window. I then felt a presence in the hall behind me as I was standing in the doorway of the room. As I began to turn to look, an investigator shouted out that she had just seen a shadow standing behind me. I stepped out into hall, but saw nothing at that point, but knew that something had been there.

There was one more major event for me at this home. I had taken two investigators into the basement. It was your standard low ceiling Michigan basement. The floor was made of dirt. I walk a few steps into an opened side room. I could still see the other two investigators as the stood on a board to stay off the wet muddy floor. We then heard what sounded like metal scrape against cement. One of the others jumped forward away from the basement stairs. I actually thought that they had fallen off the board and that that was the noise. I was wrong. She said she did not fall, but jumped away as we heard the noise. So I went to the stairs to investigate or to debunk on what the noise may had been. I find an old metal pot lid sitting on the concrete stairs. I twist it making the exact sound that we had just heard.

One final experience in Metamora. We started to do a tour out at the Metamora location, we were trying to help the client with their finances. It was a four part tour the old farmhouse built in 1900, 28 acres of farmland, Blood Road and Cry Baby Bridge. The second two are locations that are based on more of an urban legend, but still had claims of hauntings and dark history. So as part of the tour that we did, we took the investigators to Cry Baby Bridge. This urban legend as we found in our research, is found in many states around the

United States. As the group was on the bridge, I decided to walk down the road into the darkness. I had seen something in the woods. The best way that I can describe it was very inhuman in shape, size and color. The first thing that popped in my head for some reason was Elemental. It was tall and a light shade of green, no sex could be determined and no hair to be seen. Very tall and skinny. Way skinnier than anything should be. It also seemed twisted body wise. It did remind me of the White Entity in some ways and in other ways not. It crossed the road about 30 feet in front of me. I froze when I saw. It an odd and eerie feeling came over me. To see something so inhuman, especially for a second time in my life, well it is hard to explain. It is almost unbelievable to me, but I know what I saw. Being a witch and dealing with the elements and energies and such, I have no problem in believing in other types of energy forms. I believe in other realms and at some points in time or locations, that and if the timing is right, perhaps the different realms and plains of existence seep into each other. Overlap if you will. As I say, I prefer to have the hardcore evidence to back up experiences, but in this field there must be things that one cannot explain. Endless amounts of theories and ideas and sometimes things just happen that you cannot explain, and you must take them as is. What you do with these experiences is up to the individual. Another investigator thought that she had saw something as well, but was farther away and was too dark for her to tell but she had felt the same on what it may have been. There was a picture captured by one of the patrons it was a weird misty type thing in the woods surrounding the bridge. It did have a humanoid shape. It was sent to me via print out, but is very hard to see in that medium.

Sketch Of the Wood Elemental At Cry-Baby Bridge

I would like to add a story that may prove that at least at points we were dealing with the same entities. That these entities, for some reason stay on the property. That they may converse between each other or at least know of each other. Both of these sessions come from before we had started the tours out there. The first came from the March 29th 2013 investigation. An investigator went to do a session in the basement. He took another person who was there observing. He began to run the Spirit Box. The girl that was with him kept asking a lot of questions. Alot. Through the Spirit Box came a male voice saying "You're stupid." The next comes from the May 25th 2013 investigation. We were on the second floor of the home. Again, we begun to run the Spirit Box. We asked, "Who were they calling stupid at the last investigation." We started running down names. We went through about three names and there were no response. Until we reached the name of the woman who was in the basement with the investigator that first time. It was a female or perhaps a child's voice that responded. As soon as the name was spoken the reply was "That's it" How did this entity know what the male entity had said the first time? These are the types of questions that keep me searching for the answers.

The Metamora case, the tour and the people that it has brought into my life have made a great impact on me. The case remains open and I still hope to find the answers that I seek for the clients and myself.

Actual Photo: Blood Road

Actual Photo: Taken From "Cry Baby" Bridge

The Most Recent Metamora Tour

August 23rd 2014: So here we are again, the Metamora Tour/Investigation. It was going good as usual. We had set up, got everyone signed up and had just finished the history of the hauntings tour. I split the group into three smaller groups and we began the night. Now this is where things had begun to happen for me. The group headed out to the woods had just left when we discovered that we had to switch the channels on the walkie-talkies, as we were picking up on the driving part of the tour. I started my way to meet up with the wood group. As I walked down the path past the cows and pigs, I hit a divot in the ground. As I regained myself, I lifted my flashlight. Just then, right in front of me, I saw a shadow human-like, but crouched down on all fours like an animal. It was really bizarre to me the way it looked. It ran right in front of me, in a sort of gallop. I jumped back and shined my light in the direction that it went, but saw nothing. I then caught up to the group pulled my investigator aside and told him what I had seen. We then switched the channels and I headed back.

Sketch: This Is What I Saw Crossing The Path As I Was Trying To Catch Up To The Group In The Woods

I was a bit hesitant while on my way back. The shadow thing that I had saw a few moments earlier, well it was weird and I was still trying to figure it out. As I walk along the electric fence, the three cows began charging towards me. I then thought I saw one of the owners of the farm back in the field behind the cows. I thought that he was trying to coral them or something. The cows then ran off towards where I was headed. As I reached the end of the fence, I saw the owner talking to

Darlene. I then asked him if he was in the fence with the cows. He said no, he had been there with Darlene the whole time.

My final experience that night took place on the second floor boy's room. This was the room that, on prior investigations, I saw the two entities. Anyway, I was walking through the house snapping random pictures as I passed the staircase leading upstairs. Something told me to go up. As I reached the top of the stairs, a heaviness set in and I got that feeling something was up there. I stepped into the boy's room. As I stood there, I heard the metal latch on the closet door move. The door was already open, so it wasn't that it was just the handle jiggling. I then began to jump around and stomp the floor to see if I could re-create it, but it made no sound. I snapped a few more pictures and ended up leaving. Here is an interesting thing though. I was told by one of the owners that the day before the tour, she was up cleaning in the room she then heard the door latch and the door began to open by itself.

Royal Oak Michigan

January 26th 2013: This is where it may be hard to understand some things. There are parts of this case that will not be revealed due to respect and client privacy, as with many of the cases in this book, but what I will tell you will be enough to understand the case.

Let's start with the interview of the client. Myself and the case manager at the time, went to the client's house to conduct the first interview. About half way through, the feeling started. I was sitting on the couch, but could see the top of the stairs. Not physically, but in my head. Standing at the top of the stairs was an old man. A tall slender man. White disheveled hair. One feature stood out above the rest though. His nose was bulbous and red and I could see the pores in it. It was the kind of nose that you may see from a person with an alcohol problem. I of course, kept it to myself. The case manager had noticed me acting off and when we went outside after the interview was over, she asked me what I saw. I told her and we left. Actually, on my way home, the old man was in the backseat of my car. I asked him what he wanted, but as soon as I did, he was gone. I gathered up the team that following weekend and we went to the home to investigate. It turned out to be an interesting night.

The first time out, a lot of evidence was caught. Also, many encounters with the entities that were believed to be in that house. My first encounter that night was in the basement. I was sitting there doing an E.V.P. session. I then saw the old man walking down the stairs. As he reached the bottom of the stairs, it was like he kept going. His body was half way under the floor. He was just walking around as if to be looking for something. Soon after, the old woman came out from the other side of the basement. She too was half way underground. She also seemed to be looking for something. The thing that seemed odd to me was, that they did not seem to know the other one was there. They were both there for a couple of minutes and then they were both gone. Later that night, I also went down into the basement by myself. I was down there for but a moment when I heard an older lady whisper to me in my ear. I was running a digital recorder, but it was really low and hard to hear. Now we were out there several times, sorry I may get some of my nights mixed up, but I believe that was also the night that we all heard footsteps coming down the stairs. Another investigator took pictures of the stairs right after we heard them. A black mass was caught in a few different pictures. There was also a female voice caught on the recorder that night.

February 23rd 2013: The second time out was just as active. It started for me at the top of the stairs. The old man rushed me and got right in my face. He was trying to intimidate me I believe. It was very uncomfortable, but I did not back down.

He eventually left. Later that night, I caught a black mass in my photos that I took in the basement. Also in the basement, we were all sitting down there spread out. We began to hear voices but from only one side of the room. The others did not hear them. At one point, two investigators switched sides of the room and now the one could hear the voices and the other now could not.

After two investigations and more conversations with the client, I came to find out that the client, among other entities in the house, felt that it was possibly a grandfather. I took this time to tell her that I did a sketch of one of the entities in the home. I did not want to describe it at this time. I told her that I would bring it on the next evidence reveal and that if she could find a picture of him, we would compare. The time came to see if it was the same person. Was the old man I had seen the grandfather? With sketch in hand, I had her describe him. She told me that she did not remember him very well and the last time they saw him was in the hospital. She then proceeded to tell me that they were scared to go see him because of his nose, it was large and miss-colored. I asked how he had died, she told me from drinking. I was ready to show her the sketch. Although the picture that she had shown me was hard to make out and was a younger version of him, the body shape was the same. I showed her my sketch. It was very, very similar to her grandfather. The nose, the way the hair stuck up and the body shape. We believe, that among the spirits in the house, he may be one of them. Can I say a hundred percent? Of of course not, but it all seems very coincidental to me.

At this point, after more evidence was revealed, the client wanted to cleanse the house. So we then set up to do so. Being a witch, I knew what needed to be done. I took Darlene my wife and another investigator. I salted and sealed the rooms as the other investigator saged. Darlene filmed and helped out with what needed to be done. My daughter was also there and helped as well. Normally I would not have taken her, but that is just how it worked out, but the more people the more good energy. Which I believe helps with the cleansing. We did all ground and put up shields to protect ourselves. When cleansing a house, I was taught to go from the top floor, then the basement to the main floor. Back to front sealing rooms with salt after sagging as you go. You will end up at the front door and push, or sweep the entity or entities out of the house. Then seal the front door. We then cleansed the outside property. Again, I cannot guarantee anything 100 percent, but the cleansing seemed to work. Keep in mind though a cleansing may take several times.

After the cleansing, we did not really hear from the client for some time. I do check in with our clients from time to time and everything had been going fine. She then ended up contacting us several months later. She said that the activity had restarted.

We went back out to re-investigate. To be truthful, by this point, there had been some tension already building in the team. This made for a bit of a harder investigation. We pushed through and we did have some experiences. Like we heard noises and saw shadows. I also had one experience that will talk about in a bit. I also had a long talk with the client. They were supposed to do some things in order to let things go after the cleansing. These things were not done. I feel that they did not want to let go of certain things and people. I believe that the client, by doing this, may have allowed them back into her home. It may not have been purposely, but it was done never the less. Don't get me wrong, the things that this family had gone through would be hard for anyone to let go off, and rightfully so. She then said, that she was ready to try and let go of the things that she was hanging on to. She had her plan in mind. I told her if she needed anything from us that we would be there for her and her family. Although the case remains open, I have not really heard from her in a while, but I am sure that I will see them again.

Original Sketches Of the Old Man And The Woman In The Basement

There is one more short event that I have decided to add to this. This experience comes from the last time that I was out there. I did not collect any evidence to support this experience to the client, as I did with the sketch of the Old Man. It is much more my theory, but I will now write about it.

I was on the upper floor with another investigator. We had heard something that we could not explain. As we started to look around to see what it was, something told me to open the door to the attic storage area. It was small but long and dark. As I opened the door, I got a cool gust of wind that hit me. This was summer, the attic should have been warmer than the rest of the house. As I stuck my camera in, I was very uneasy. It felt like something was going to swipe my hand. Then I saw it the face. Whatever this was was very old. I became flush and broke out into a sweat. I also started to experience a shortness of breath. I move back from the door as quick as I could. The other investigator must have seen my reaction and asked what had happened. I proceeded to tell her. Now this is where my theories come in, as I said I felt that this entity was very old and not connected to the house, but the people. This is just the feeling that I had picked up on when I saw it.

Sketch Of the Attic Creeper

Actual Photo: Of the Black Mass Caught In The Basement

Actual Photo: Number Two Of Black Mass In The Basement

Actual Photo: Of the Black Mass On The Stairs. This Was Taken After Several Of the Investigators Heard Footsteps On The Stairs Including Myself

Actual Photo Of The [illegible] Stairs On The Right. This Was Taken After Several of the [illegible] Heard Footsteps On The Stairs Including Myself

Fort Wayne, Detroit

In 1840 at the point on the Detroit River closest to Canada, the United States Army began surveying local farms for the placement of new artillery post. A five point star fort was set to be built. This new fort would be Detroit's third.

Starting in 1948 the fort was given to Detroit in pieces. Over the next 28 years, they would come to own the entire fort with the exception of nine acres which are still occupied by the Army Corps of Engineers. To this day you can visit the original 1848 limestone barracks building 1845 Star Fort which was renovated in 1861 the restored Commanding Officer's house, Spanish

American War guard house, and the Tuskegee Airmen Museum. Today Fort Wayne is coming back and the preservation is still underway. Every year that I went back, there was always a new building or location restored and opened to us for investigation.

Haunted History

There have been apparitions seen on the grounds such as what seemed to be a guard walking the wall. Entities have been seen in the buildings and case mates as well. Voices are heard throughout different locations of the property. I myself have also heard other teams and caught many E.V.P.'s here. There has also been reports of doors slamming. I once again, have witnessed the doors slamming for myself.

This is a location that I have investigated many times. Probably the location that I have investigated the most. My first E.V.P. that I have ever caught came from this location. It was mine and Darlene's second official place that we had investigated. We have had many experiences here and I have caught evidence every time that we have went. Hell, one summer we went down there five times.

I will try and keep these in some kind of order, but like I said, we were down there a lot.

After our trip to Mansfield, Ohio we were hooked. Almost instantly when we had got back. We started looking for the next place to go. We were far from thoughts of a team at this point, but still wanted to go on investigations. Darlene came across a fort in Detroit that were holding "Ghost Hunts". This was in our own backyard, not more than twenty minutes away. The next day at work I had approached my friend Keri that had taken us on our first investigation. Unfortunately this time, she could not make it. So I and my wife booked the night for the two of us.

So the night arrives and I am once again excited beyond what I can explain. We pull up to the location and once again I was in awe. The size of the location was incredible. We met the team that was running this event. We later became great friends with this set of people. We were taken on a tour of the grounds and then let loose to investigate.

We started in the first case mate. This is a tunnel like structure built into the ground. It has both gun and cannon ports. This is where I actually caught my first E.V.P. and it was actually two. One right after another. The first was a gravelly voice that said "This One." The second sounded like a younger female and it said "They're After Me."

When I first heard these in review, I could not believe it. The feeling you get when you know who is in the area with you, knowing who is talking, and you get another voice caught in your conversation. Well I have tried to explain it to other people, but you just cannot. You have to be there experience it for yourself. Anyway, we then headed to the barracks where the soldiers had slept. Now we had a good time in there, but really no experiences or evidence was caught. After that, we headed to the jailhouse. Here we caught one of Darlene's favorite E.V.P.'s. We sat down in the "drunk tank" side and started the recorder. I introduced ourselves as I always do, but after I said "This is Brian and Darlene in the jailhouse" the response came back in a whisper saying "Darlene who?" Which by the way, is one of Darlene pieces of evidence. The night ended strange with some drunk guys crashing there car into the security station and smashing it to bits. They were not from the tour. Thankfully no one was in it. We were put on a short lock down as they searched the grounds for these men, but they were not there.

Actual Photo: Of What Appears To Be A Mist Forming. The Two Dark Human Shapes At The Bottom Are Two Other Investigators

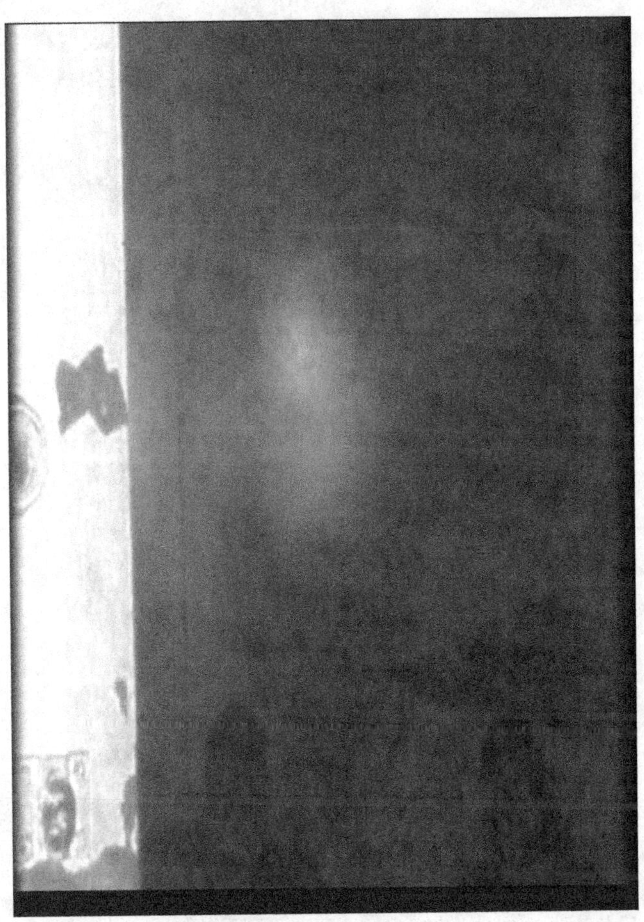

Actual Photo: Of A Weird Floating Anomaly. At First I Thought It To Be Dust, And It Still Could Be, But Its Shape Is Off And It Has The Strange "Skull" Likes Appearance. I Do Not Claim This To Be A Ghost. Just Found It Strange And Decided To Share It. This May Just Be A Great Example Of How Dust Will Matrix Into Something.

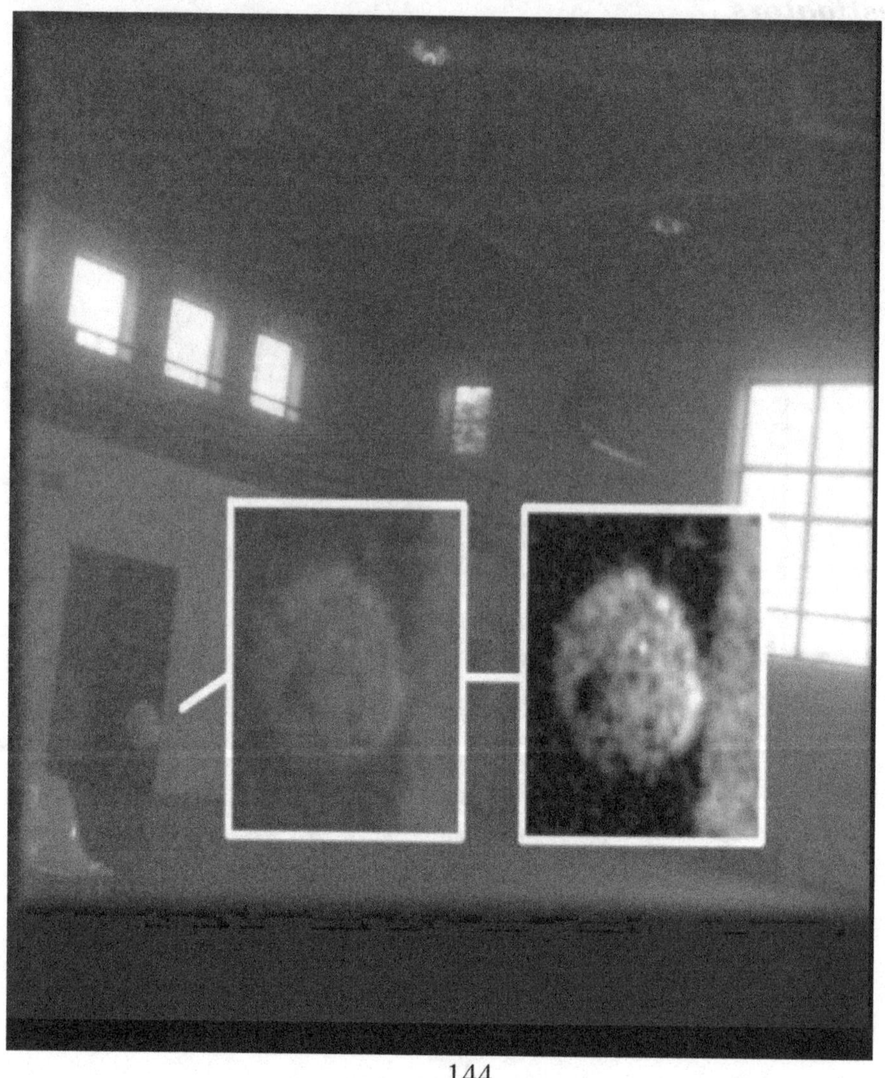

Actual Photo: Of What Appears To Me To Be An Entity Or Entities In The Window.

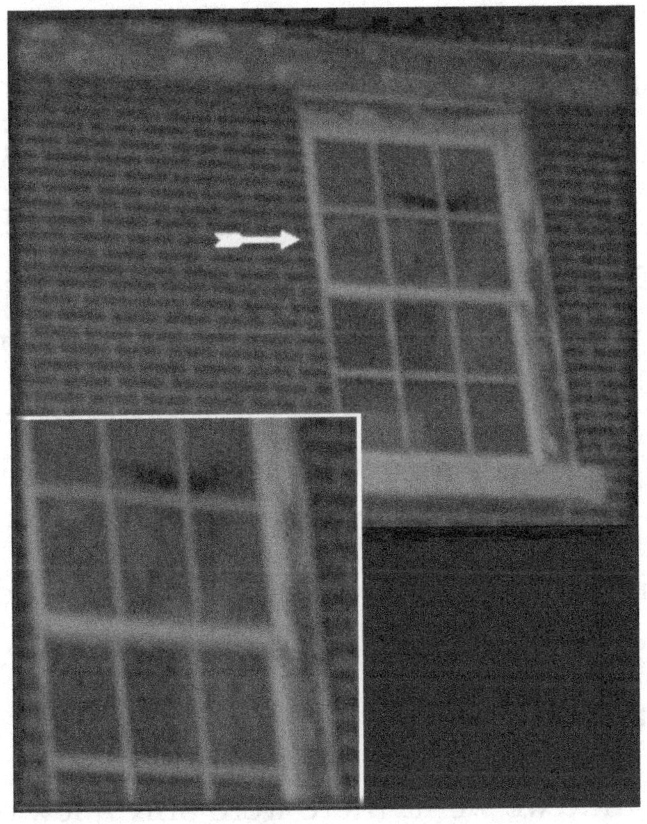

The next time we decided to go back, we were able to take the original people that took us on our first investigation in Mansfield Ohio, among others. This time there were no on hand experiences. Although we did capture evidence. At the end of the night there were only a few of us left. Now to be honest, this was before the team and I was very excited to be doing this. I still am very excited to do this still, but I have grown and are now more able to control myself. So much so, that I kept taking off from the people that I was with. At the beginning of this paranormal journey I did that a lot, especially to my wife Darlene and for that I apologize. Anyway, she had left for the night the remaining four of us went into the gym area to do a final session. Now I have this evidence both on 8mm and digital recorder. I caught a young female voice plain as day saying "Where you at?" Now there are no children allowed on this tour as with most. On the video footage you can see who is in the room; me, my friend Keri, and her two daughters. This is still one of the best E.V.P.'s that I have ever caught.

The next time we went, there were only a few of us. We had been investigating for a while that night. We ended up in the barracks. Second floor, in a room that we had dubbed "Emily's Room" This is when this location became truly special to me. It started with the first time that I ever got a response on the flashlight. It was dead on each time. I think that the first time that it came on, well I am surprised that I did not have to change my shorts. I could not believe it. The only words to describe it was pure excitement. After a long while of communication with the flashlight, I had asked "If you are not Emily, please scream your name into one of the red lights placed throughout the room. It did. We had three digital recorders placed all around the room, only one picked up a name Burnett. With only one recorder picking this up, well made it that much better. We later did some research confirming that there were several people named Burnett that had at some point, been at this location. After that I had stood up and began to walk around and stretch my legs. I had the video camera in hand. As I got closer to the door, I felt something push the back of my hand. So much so that the camera that I was holding moved. The best way that I can describe the feeling is it was like when you stand up too fast. My whole body became warm and flushed. There was a strange calmness about it though. I quickly shouted out that I had thought something touched me. Am I sure that this is truly what it was, not a hundred percent, but my intuition says it was an entity giving me physical contact. I could not sit back down and went about asking more questions. I then said, that while all of this was impressive could they do something like slam a door. From down to hall at the other end of the barracks you could hear a door slam in the distance. We did not believe this to be true. I mean, how often does that work in this field? So I said what we always say "If that was you can you do it again?" Probably within 20 to 30 feet of the room that we were in, another door slammed loudly. Again, disbelief. Also some colorful language may have been used in excitement. I walk up to the doorway of the room. I stood there frozen. I could not force myself to leave the room. This had become real. It was much more than I had ever expected. I did zoom the camera down the hall to see if I could see anything and I did not see anybody or anything in the hall. Now a days it would be a different story. I would have ran down there to see, but that night I will admit that even though there was excitement, I was starting to get slightly freaked out. Keri stepped over and decided to go in the hall she made a few steps out and came back. She later told me when she was out there in the hall alone she thought to herself, "What the Hell are you doing?" She re-entered the room. We went on to investigate for but a few moments and then decided to regroup. We got down to the outside of the barracks. There we saw a group of the people that were running the tour. If you know these people, than you know that they are very trustworthy. I asked them if they had seen anybody come in or leave the barracks as of late. They said no, they had seen no one but us. They then proceeded to radio to home base to see who was left on the grounds. The call came back that we were the only ones left on the tour. The others had checked out much earlier. The time frame that the last ones had checked out was way before we ever went into the barracks. This was the confirmation that we needed to tell us that the events that had just taken place was most likely paranormal. We ended up closing out the tour, but nothing happened again on that night.

We have since then been back several times with several different people. Every time that we have gone, we have walked out every time with some kind of evidence. Even on the few nights that we thought that there was no activity, we still caught something.

The last time that we investigated there, was the time that I encountered the White Entity mentioned before. I will start from the beginning though. We were there for about a quarter of the night and it seemed as if nothing was going on. We decided to investigate one of the case mates We sat for a bit, I was not feeling anything. I then decided to open myself. Soon after, it worked. I saw a soldier sitting on the steps that led out of the case mate I too was sitting on the steps. At the time the entity was a few steps above me. It was a tan uniform and he was wearing a wedge hat. I am not sure if this is what he was doing, but it seemed as if he winked at me. Like this was our secret, that he was in there with us. I then leaned over to Darlene and whispered in her ear as to what I was seeing and feeling. He was then soon gone.

Sketch Of the Case Mate Entity

We went through out to the different locations, but I did not see anything. Until we once again reached the barracks. As not to make you re-read the same stories, I will just write a brief reminder as to the events that took place next. We were on the third floor at one of the ends of the building. This is where I started to pick up on the soldier in green. The one who turned bloody. Now why he did this, I do not know. Then the encounters with the White Entity would take place. Including seeing it in the first case mate I had left that night very confused on what I was seeing and what had happened that night. I am not sure even to this day what all of this meant.

Sketch Of the Green Suited Soldier That I saw Right Before The White Entity

The next time that we were out was for an event that was taking place there. I believe it was the biggest "Ghost Hunt" to take place. There were hundreds of people there. Into The AfterLife Paranormal was one of the sponsors at this event. I had reserved the end of the barracks where I had the previous experiences. Each sponsor had a location on the premises and a technique that they were to share with the groups that would be coming through the night. Ours was E.V.P. sessions. We were to show and teach on how we did them. Such as no whispering and tagging noises as not to confuse them with something that may be something paranormal. The night was going great, in fact it was one of the more fun things that I had done with the original team. We were in between sessions when I had seen a little girl standing in the area where I had first encountered the White Entity. I approached her and sat on the floor. To be on her level. I reached out to her to come over to me. She was young with braided pick-tails. She eventually made her way over to me. As I reached out for her hand, a great sadness hit me. My eyes once again began to water. Not as to cry, it is different and hard to explain. We sat for what seemed like a long while. The next group had entered the room. I looked over at them. As I turned back to the girl she was gone. I once again shared the experience with Darlene. Now I have since then heard stories of others that have seen a young girl in this building. I do wonder though, is this the same girl that I have been capturing on the digital recorder? I wonder. **Note:** One of the investigators that evening had captured an E.V.P. of a young child. I was in on the session, so I know that it was genuine. Unfortunately the E.V.P. was supposed to be sent to me, but never was.

Sketch Of the Young Girl In The Barrack

The very last time that I was down at the fort. Myself and Darlene were volunteers and helping out with the tour. We did not investigate for ourselves, but did get to help out with the new program that was added to the tour. Investigate with the investigators. This gave newer people a chance to see some of the techniques used by the people who have been doing it longer. While in the case mate, I heard someone whispering. I tagged it as one of the tour guides. The other tour guide heard it as well. As I tagged it, the one I thought said it said

"That wasn't me" in fact she did not even hear it. We also had a weird light thing happen. It seemed as if the light on the K2 meter was moving. Now this will happen while staring at a light in the dark. We even tested that. The weird thing was that everyone in that case mate and there were about 25 of us saw it moving at the same time. Still, I cannot call this paranormal. It was just a part of the experience. For the rest of the night we sat by the fire discussing equipment and answering questions that came to us by the patrons. Later that night, after the tour myself and one of the regulars that work there, Stephanie, were locking down the barracks. She was at one end and me at the other. We were the only two people in there. I was on the staircase locking the door on the second floor when I heard noises from the first floor. I yelled down to see if it was the other person. Someone answered me, but I could not understand what they had said. I thought it was Stephanie, who was locking down with me. I immediately went downstairs. I saw nobody. I began to walk towards the other end of the building. About half way down I met up with her. She was not even close to me when I heard this stuff going on. I then told her about It, and she says that it was definitely not her and I believe her. She, like her team is very trustworthy.

Unfortunately this was the last time that I was down at the fort. The tours as of now are on a break. Hopefully one day, I will be able to get back down there to investigate.

Clinton Township Michigan

This case comes from one of Darlene's co-workers. It started off with a picture that they had sent Darlene. The client was taking a picture of very small child hand prints on her mirror. The odd thing is there are no young kids in the home. The other odd thing is, that in the picture there is an apparition. It appears as it is coming through the bed. Of course we were skeptical. We had her try and re-create the photo and resend them to us. We even had her wait and try it at the same time the next day. She sent several pictures and nothing matched. That is when we had decided to go and try to re-create it ourselves. We showed up at the client's house and began to take several pictures hundreds in. We could not produce the same image as the original.

This Is the Original Client Picture and The Best Re-Creation That Took

After trying for quite some time to re-create it, we started the investigation. This was going to be a short one. Almost like an interview investigation, just to see if there was anything to be caught as evidence. We started in the master bedroom. We did run the Spirit Box for a short time. We did capture a few things in audio, but the visual that we had caught was awesome. We caught a black mass on camera moving across the room in several different pictures. In fact, in one picture it looks like a hand trying to block out the lenses. We were scheduled to return, but after we had left everything in the home quieted down. The client did not want to stir it up again. Maybe perhaps the reveal of the evidence, as I know myself, makes it become too real. Which of course is understandable. We are still in contact with the client and if they need us to return we will.

Actual Photo : Of the Shadow That Moved Across The Room

Actual Photo : Of the Shadow As It Was Getting Bigger

Actual Photo : Of the Shadow This Is The One That Looks Like A Hand To Me

Actual Photo Of The Shadow This Is The One That

Looks Like A Hand To Me

Historic Starr House In Royal Oak Michigan

Brief History: A Farmer from upstate New York, named Orson Starr, was a well-known manufacturer. Mr. Starr and his family made their living by producing both bricks and cowbells. The cowbells are now sought after by collectors of antiques.

In 1845, Mr. Starr built a wooden frame house two miles north of what is now downtown Royal Oak. This home was lived in by the descendants of the Starr Family until the late 1970s. It was then purchased by the City of Royal Oak.

The Orson Starr House is now listed in Michigan's State Register of Historic Sites and has been designated as a historic district.

Now there is not a lot of paranormal history that has been documented at this place. There had been at least one paranormal investigator there before us, along with a few newspaper clippings that I found about his visit. When we went in, there were claims of the feeling of being watched all of the time, noises and voices and of course that thing that you will see moving from the corner of your eye. I myself have captured E.V.P.'s, heard audio voices in the basement, along as seeing an apparition of an old man in the basement as well. Who seemed to be a bit angry. I also felt a woman's presence and heard her voice. There also may be an entity of a child lurking about.

For More Information Please Visit: www.ci.royaloak.mi.us/portal/community-links/historical-commission/orson-starr-house

November 18th 2013: This was actually my second investigation at this location. I will fill you in the first case a little, and how it was cut short. I was invited by another local team to join them in their investigation. This was the time in between the old team and the new team. Where I did witness an old man in the basement, it was brief. A few moments of him watching us in the basement. It then became more of a feeling of what he was feeling. He seemed to be very grouchy. I do not know if it was because we were in the home or if that is how he was in life. At the second investigation I came across a picture that I did not see the first time. It seems to be the same man, or very similar. Anyway, the second part of the investigation, for myself, took place on the second floor. I was paired with an investigator from the other team and we ran our session. After the session ended, we headed downstairs. I made it down to where the equipment was stored. The next thing I know I heard a loud noise. The other investigator was laying at the bottom of the stairs. I think that everyone was in shock for what seemed like forever. Once everyone had realized what had happened, we all ran over to assist her. She had broken her hip. After a while, I ended up leaving and that was the end of that night, and understandably so. I did although, capture some E.V.P.'s from the basement that night.

March 29th 2014: Now let's jump ahead to the more current time that I investigated there. I went in with the new team. At the time that I am writing this, we are 13 members strong. I was only in for a few seconds and I had got that shiver down my spine. A few moments later, a few of the investigators had said what a heavy feeling. That they were feeling it in the house. We proceeded to set up base camp and run cameras. I split the teams into smaller groups and they began to investigate.

The first team headed to the basement. The second team went to the second floor. My team sat the first session out at home base. We did not want to cause contamination of possible evidence. The basement team was getting direct responses to their flashlight session. Again, I know that there is a debate on whether this is truly paranormal or not, but when you get direct responses or they switch between flashlights when you ask it is a little harder to dismiss. After about a forty minute session, I went to rotate the teams. I did not get too much info from the upstairs team, but the basement team had told me about the session with the flashlight. I was getting ready to send the teams out again when one of the investigators became overwhelmed with sadness. She began to cry. She quickly removed herself from the house to regroup herself. Myself and Darlene followed her out to make sure that she was OK. After a few moments, she was able to regain herself and we re-entered the location. It was at this point that I began to feel the old man again. You see, while I was at the DVR at home base I had opened myself up for communication. He was there in the doorway leading into the kitchen, which led to the basement, where we headed. He was there for but a moment and was gone. Just a reminder, I do not mention this to the investigators, I only will mention too few as not to influence.

So we hit the basement and set up our equipment along with two separate flashlights purple and black. Right away we started to get direct responses on the flashlights, and again it was going back and forth as we had asked. At one point I and another investigator both heard a whisper. I had asked if anyone had heard that and she said yes. It was at this point that her husband, another investigator, had said that he had heard something as well. He just did not want to say anything. He thought he was crazy. A short time after that, we all heard a woman's voice come from the corner of the basement. We all turned our heads in the same direction at the same time. That is how I knew before I had asked them if they had heard it. Of course, they had confirmed that they did. I radioed up to home base to see if anyone was in the kitchen or by the basement stairs. The answer was no. A few moments later, home base called down to us and asked if we had done the Shave And A Haircut bit. That's a knocking that we do hoping for a response with a knocking back. I told them no. They then proceeded to tell me that it sounded like it something was tapping it on the window. We ended the session shortly after that and headed upstairs.

Once again I had the teams rotate. My team headed to the second floor. We were up there for almost a half an hour. We had no feelings and no responses to anything that we were trying. So we headed to home base. I was standing there for a brief moment at home base when I was hit with a crowdedness. That's the best way that I can explain it. It felt like the old man was there, but he had others with him. Although I did not see them, I felt an older female entity a child and another adult male. Suddenly I hear a screaming from the basement. I run down there to find yet another investigator crying, but it was much more intense than the investigator from earlier. I grabbed her hand and told her that she needed to leave the house. I then proceeded to help her outside. She was eventually able to calm herself and re-enter the house. I decided to do one final session on the main floor with the whole team. A lot of the feeling in the house had left at this point. I thanked the entities in the house for allowing us into their home, I closed myself, we packed up and headed home. Later that night is when I had the dream that was mentioned above. I guess from this particular case. I learned that I need to make sure that my team protects themselves better before we enter a location. We should probably do it as a team. Even now there is still and will always be lessons to be learned.

I have since reviewed the evidence from this last time that we had investigated. While I am still awaiting for the other investigators to reveal if they have caught anything, I myself have caught some possible Spirit Box hits.

I would like to add that we have been getting a lot of cases in this area and strangely enough, most of them have been connecting to this location and the people who had lived there. After some research from one of our investigators and historians, we have found that the last three cases that we have had are all linked to this historical site.

Sketch Of the Older Man That I Saw In The Basement

Private Home In Clawson Michigan

December 12th 2013: This case connects to the case of the historical house in Royal Oak that we had done. We were called out to this case to investigate for the family. They claimed to be experiencing a lot of paranormal activity. A lot of it towards the wife, although they all were seeing things and hearing things she was being touched.

This was our first case with some of the new investigators and just to add, set up and the sessions went very well. We started in the basement. We ran our usual equipment, but for some reason we decided to run the Ovilus. The Ovilus is a piece of equipment that has words set in it at different power levels. It is believed that a spirit can choose from these words depending on how much energy that they put into it. Other theories suggest that spirits and other paranormal entities may be able to alter our environment such as electromagnet frequencies, temperature, etc. to be able to use this device. I have never used any Ovilus session for evidence until now, but first I will tell you about the woman being as I saw her first.

We were all sitting around the basement, I could see the staircase leading back upstairs. Suddenly a woman appears. She is all twisted and descending the stairs almost spider-like. She was mostly bald, but had patches of thin blonde hair. She wore a peach dress. She was very creepy in appearance. We were there for but a moment. My questions began to change, as they usually do when a spirit reveals them to me. I started to ask what her means of death may have been. The hair loss was my main focus, thinking that this had something to do with her death. At this point I neither had, nor told anyone of this entity. Although later I did tell the team, but not the clients. The case was still building and again I do not like to influence. I also wanted to make sure that there would be evidence to back it up.

After that "meeting" a strange thing came through the Ovilus the word "Spirits." I quickly asked how many spirits and it immediately said "Seven." I have never had a direct response from this device. It then said "Kate." Now here is where the connection from the historical house comes in. After much research we found out the son of the owner of the historical house owned the property that the Clawson home now sits on. It was the son's farm. Even more bizarre, his daughter had died on the land she was about 8 or 9 we could not find the cause of death. The death certificate was written on pencil and was hard to read. Her name was Katheryn.

After the basement session, we headed upstairs. There we had quite a good flashlight session with whom we believed to be "Kate." We ended the night and went home. After review, we did capture some evidence. After the evidence review for the client we did a follow up. Everything seemed to have calmed down for a while.

March 8th 2014: We were contacted a few months later, the activity had returned. We went back with a smaller crew there were only three of us. The rest of the investigators had fell ill. We went through the night doing sessions. We even had the female home owner help out. Of course we only do this if the owners feel comfortable and agree to do so. We would never put a client in harm's way. One off her new claims was that she was getting disturbed while in her bed. So we stationed a DVR camera on her and the bed. We had her lay there alone to see if anything would happen. We monitored the whole session and nothing happened. The house this time did feel different. Calm. We did not experience or capture any evidence this time.

The clients were still feeling uncomfortable. So with their permission, I suggested that I bring in another paranormal team. I wanted to get others ideas and theories of what may be going on. Maybe they would have better luck than we did the last time that we were out. This team I had been on investigations with and trusted them fully. In fact when this team unfortunately disbanded, for personal reasons, many of them came over to Into The AfterLife Paranormal and I was happy to receive them. Anyway, that team agreed and went out to the home to investigate. They too caught some evidence. This case remains open to this day.

Sketch Of the Woman On The Stairs

Southfield Michigan

March 7th 2014: I was contacted by this client with claims of seeing shadow people, hearing things and physical contact. They have been with some entity or entities wherever they move and it has been with them for many years. Once again, there is much more to this story, but must be kept confidential. By the time that they contacted me, the activity had been getting worse. We picked a date and I got the team together for the investigation. We went in as always and got all the equipment set up. We then proceeded to start our sessions. It is a tri-level home and we were in the lower level. For some reason this time, everything seemed to be in a state of chaos. Maybe it was just me, but the Spirit Box that was running seemed exceptionally loud and there were about three investigators messing with it. The clients were in the mid-level, which was the main floor. They were shuffling around in the kitchen. During this time I happened to look up to the landing at the top of the stairs. There I saw a very tall black humanoid shape. It seems twisted, almost snake-like. It was there for a few moments and as soon as I raised my camera to snap some pictures, it was gone. I did not mention this to anyone. Although we did conduct a session with the clients and during that I did ask if anyone that they knew who had died, that they had thought may have been there and was very tall. They said no, not really. Although one friend that had died was taller than the rest. I do not think that this was him.

We finished the investigation and left. I did tell Darlene when I got home that night about the tall shadow being at the top of the stairs.

We reviewed all of the evidence and caught nothing. I was not going to say anything else about the shadow being, not even to the team. I needed some kind of proof, evidence wise to prove that something may have been there. I will never just give client speculations of something that *may* or *may not* be there with any hardcore proof to back me up.

A while after we told them that we had found nothing, they called us again. Although the activity was still there, it had calmed down. Not enough for them to be at ease though. They wanted another more intense investigation and a house cleansing. I told them that we would do one or the other in a single night. That a cleansing in itself could take a few hours. They decided to do the investigation first and then if need be a cleansing after. They had also asked us to get them some supplies such as holy water and sage among other things, they wanted on hand just in case.

April 19th 2014: Return to Southfield. We arrived and went over what we had planned for the night. We were going to do an investigation, but with the OK of the clients were going to do a land cleansing. This takes much less time than a home cleansing. They agreed and we proceeded. I sent the first of the investigators into the location. I sat in the van. This is when and where I decided to open myself. Almost immediately after opening, I saw a black shadow peek at me from behind a small brick wall. It did not leave when I saw it. It was like it wanted me to know that it knew why we were there. Interesting to me, and I do not know for sure if this is the case, but the inside team said that it was very quiet while they were in there. They were in for a little over a half hour. Did the shadow being outside cause for them to have a quiet session in the home? I wonder.

Soon it was my turn to go in. With my group of investigators we headed up to the master bedroom. It started for me by seeing movement in the bathroom that was connected between the two bedrooms. So much so that I stood up and went to look around to see what it may be. I did not find anything. There were also no windows in the bathroom for outside interference. One of the investigators began to run her Spirit Box. Some interesting things seem to come through, such as the client's names when asked for. At this point I was kneeling on the far side of the bed, head down. I started to receive these bizarre images in my head. Even though my head was down with eyes closed I was seeing several weird death scenes and images taking place in the other room. Something told me to lift my head. I could see out the door and down the hall into the other bedroom. Sitting there was a black shadow person. It blocked out the white of the mattresses. I do not usually do this, but I found myself shouting out to what I had just seen. Of course then it was gone. We called in the other group to join us and continued with the session. I seemed to myself to be out of it. I was so into the thoughts in my head. Now it is hard to remember about what I was even thinking about. I felt lost. I would snap in and out of it. Finally, I decided that we should end the session and take a break. It was for but a few moments and we started again on the main floor. Everyone sat in the living room area. I sat at the dining room table. Once again as the session was running, I became lost in my thoughts. This has been to date, the only time that I had felt like something was trying to get inside my head, or possibly attach itself to me. I did not feel like myself. After entering the home, after I had opened myself, I actually began to feel threatened and decided that I better close myself. As I did, it seemed more difficult to push everything out and close the gates in my mind. Once I did I seen what was trying to get inside my head. The black mass, now with these deep red eyes was standing outside the locked gates and shaking them. Trying to get into my head. This has been the only time, and that includes the White Entity, that I have felt this. The feeling of something trying to get into my head and I did not like it. I was able to snap out of it again. To this point I was not even participating in the session, but asked what color eyes do you have to the Spirit

Box. It did not answer. At this point everything seemed to die down and we decided to pack it up. If we did not end up ending this session, I was ready to step out. If for anything but to regain my thoughts. I was actually starting to feel better. We packed up spoke with the clients and explained how to use the supplies that they had asked for. We then went outside to begin the land cleansing. We proceeded with the ceremony provided to us from one of our investigators. If this does not help we will return to do a full house cleansing. When finished, we left. As of now we have not finished the review, but the case remains open. At this point, I have yet to tell the clients of the black shadow being. When the time is right though, I will.

Sketch Of the Black Shadow At The Top Of the Stairs

Sketch Of the Entity That Was Trying To Get Into My Head

May 3rd 2014: The night before we were contacted by the client, even though we have not caught any evidence and I had nothing to prove the shadow entity. The clients had felt like it was worse in the home. The client had once again been touched in the bed and were still seeing "The Presence" as they kept calling it.

We set up for May 3rd for some of the team to go out and perform a full house cleansing. Again, this is no guarantee to rid the property of this entity, but hopefully it will help. If not, we will take the next step and help them find a clergy to come in and bless the home and them, as I strongly believe that this entity is an Inhuman Spirit and attached to the clients.

May 3rd 2014: The team went out and cleansed the home. Although some weird and/or coincidental things had happened, such as the sage would not stay lit, which of course can happen, and even though the fire system was shut off at the panel the alarm kept going off, and a blind fell and hit one of the investigators. Never the less, the home was cleansed and the clients feel as if there has been something lifted and a lighter feeling in the house.

June 20th 2014: So we had got a call from the client telling us that the night before they had suffered from three attacks. So we set up to go out and perform another cleansing. Unfortunately, I at the time had got really sick and was having problems with my leg so I unable to attend. Now here is something that may be coincidental, while at the Double Header Investigation in Ohio, I notice that the Black Shadow entity was still lurking about in my head. That was two weeks before the clients had called. The next weekend on a Saturday night, I released the Black Shadow from myself and forbid it to return. That was one week before the clients called back. Now did it go back to the home in Southfield? I do not know, but it is something to think about. Although I still feel a residue of sorts lingering in my mind of it, I believe it to be gone from myself and from what the team members that performed the new cleansing said, from the home as well. Side note, when something has been attached to someone as long as the clients' claim they have been dealing with this, it is not going to be so easy to get rid of, so at this point all we can do is wait and see.

As of now, after the final cleansing, the clients seem to be doing well. Hopefully this case will remain closed for them.

Ohio Double Header

Darlene and I were invited to join a group of friends and fellow paranormal investigators on a duo location investigation. The investigators came from another local Michigan team, MPI and a few from the Ohio area. Both locations are located in Ohio. The first night we would spend the night investigating the Twin City Opera House and the second night at Prospect Place. I had never been to the Opera House and this would be my third time back to Prospect Place. These investigations were much more relaxed with minimal equipment. What we like to call "Going In Old School." The term comes from how it is when you first start in this field, you do not have a bunch of fancy equipment and set ups. You run with what you have and rely a lot on your instincts. For me this trip was fantastic. It was a chance to investigate with a team and people that I have respected since I had started this paranormal journey.

Twin City Opera House June 6th/7th 2014:

Brief History: The doors of the Opera House Theater had opened to the public in 1892, but the building really had its beginnings several years earlier than that. By the end of the 1880's, the majority of the McConnelsville council thought the town needed a much more suitable place to house the village government. The council had employed an architect named H. C. Lindsay to prepare plans for the New Town Hall and Opera House. The building was going to be three stories high and it would cost about $16,000. The Town Hall would have a tower that would rise 108 feet above the sidewalks of McConnelsville. The formal opening was held on Saturday, May 28, 1892. The opening was to be a grand affair. The program for the evening was the Arion Opera Company's performance of Gilbert and Sullivan's "The Mikado." The cast the crew and the orchestra numbered nearly one hundred in all. All eight hundred seats that were then available in the auditorium were sold. Over the years the Opera House has accommodated an endless variety of performers and celebrities.

Haunted History: Not only have apparitions been seen and E.V.P.'s caught, but footsteps have been heard and odd cold spots felt. Music, singing and piano notes have also been heard. In fact, stories of the hauntings have gone back to the 60's.

For more information please visit: www.twincityoperahouse.com

We arrived to the Opera House later in the night and met up with the others in the group. We then headed over to meet the group of people running it. They gave us a brief history/paranormal tour, telling us some of the sightings that had taken place there. As I said before, a lot of times I do not like to get a whole lot of information as not to be influenced on what I may come across. So I went and walked around with a few of the other investigators while most of the speaking was going on. The place most certainly had an eerie feeling about it, as if you were being watched from the shadows especially in the area under the stage.

Soon the tour was over and we split into smaller groups, me and Darlene headed off with another investigator from the other team to the catwalk above the stage. Right away we started to receive some odd K2 hits. I am still not sure what they were from, seeing as the meter was sitting close to the floor on a wooden box there was no EMF's surrounding the area, which we had scanned before the session. It was at this point that I saw what appeared to be a lengthy shadow person on the small part of the catwalk, directly across from us. I did not mention this being as I was investigating with new people and I like to have proof to back me up. It had also passed through my mind that this looked very similar to the attachment that I had picked up from the Southfield case. It was still with me I believe. We finished the session and went to the different locations throughout the Opera House, which included the sub-basement, stage and upper balcony. I never did see the shadow person again that night. I myself also did not witness anymore activity that night, but the evidence is still in review so we will see. As I always say, you cannot control the spirits. It is up to them when they are willing to communicate.

Sketch Of the Black Shadow Entity That I Saw At The Opera House

Prospect Place June 7th/8th:

Now I have a deep respect for Prospect Place and the entities that reside there. As I have stated before, with the experiences that I have had with them, they changed my way of investigating. I was really looking forward to getting back there.

We arrived early that day and ended up hanging out in the nearby town. Soon after, we headed back and were able to get into the location. As we pulled in, I saw the awe in the other investigators faces. I had this first time that I saw the location and still do. We met with the owner, signed in and began to settle in. I walked around the building and started to receive that buzzing feeling which I did not receive the night before. There was definitely a weird energy at the location. It seemed like it was taking forever for the investigating to begin. Just as I was thinking that, one of the investigators suggested that we go up into the attic and begin. Still being daylight, shouldn't not matter. I agreed, because again, as I said before, if a location is haunted, it is haunted at both day and night. So four of us ended up in the attic. We ran a long session, but did not really receive any hits or activity. That came later in the basement and in the attic.

The Basement:

During the first session in the attic, nothing was picked up on so we decided to move to the basement. We set up equipment throughout. I was down at the far end with a few investigators, including Darlene. There were more investigators in the well room. The things that were to happen next was what we call a chain of events. First, myself and Darlene both heard what sounded like a knocking or a possible rock being thrown down a side hall. I quickly got up and went down the small hall. I searched around, but saw nothing. I sat back down and one of the investigators started her Spirit Box. After a while into the session, we picked up a full name that was related to the location. Shortly after that, my REM pod went off. This had been on the whole time and had made no noise or did not light up. It ran solid for at least 30-40 seconds. This made the other investigators that were in the well area come down to us. Once the REM Pod shut off, one of the investigators from the well area told us that right before the REM Pod went off, she had seen a shadow about four feet tall shoot down the hall towards us. Was this the spirit who set off the equipment? Going by the size of it, was it the girl whose body was kept in the basement after her tragic fall from the balcony? Or was it the woman whose name we had just heard on the Spirit Box. I do not know for sure, but it is something to think about.

We did get some direct flashlight answers after that. We began trying to figure out who it was, but that is when I had made this point. Even if the flashlight hits are true and it seems that we are talking to a certain entity, how do we know that they are who they say they are. It could be telling us that it is the little girl to get us to trust and feel more at ease, but truly be something dark and malevolent. That is something else to think about and something else to keep in mind at all investigations. Slowly the investigators began to go back upstairs. Soon the rest of us would join them.

Sketch Of the Basement Area At Prospect Place

The Attic

We decided to head back up to the attic this time. The whole group went up there. One of the investigators had some period ballroom music on her phone. She played it. I then decided to ask Darlene for a dance. We do this to hopefully stir up some paranormal activity. Doing a re-enactment of something that may have taken place in the location, such as dancing in the ballroom. We danced for a few moments and then sat back down. It was a short time after this that I began to see what appeared to be a shadow person. It first appeared to be on the wall behind Darlene. It then moved up closer to her. It did run through my mind that perhaps it was asking her to dance. Seeing how we just were dancing and then I saw it approach her. I asked if someone was standing behind Darlene and everyone said no. They asked me what I was seeing and I told them. That was about the extent of the activity that had happened to me up in the attic, but that was good enough for me. We then went to set up on the second floor.

Sketch Of the Attic Entity

The Second Floor

The whole group of us ended up on the second floor. We were spread out at the far end where the balcony is. We all had our equipment spread out, including my digital recorder. At one point during an E.V.P. session, I heard a whispery voice. At first I had thought it was one of the investigators out in the hall, but when I had asked, they told me that no one had said anything. We did end up sleeping on the second floor, but that was about the extent of activity that I personally experienced. Although I did awake early in the morning and headed downstairs to the restroom and I did get the eerie feeling as I walked down the stairs. Maybe it was the feeling of being up alone, walking through the house or perhaps I was not alone and that was the feeling that I was picking up on.

Although the extent of the activity this trip was not as active as my first trip to Prospect Place, I understand why. I believe from my first trip there was so that I could partially understood the feelings of the entities of Prospect Place. If that makes sense.

All in all, this trip was fantastic. The two locations were great and the company was even better.

Waverly Hills Sanatorium : Louisville Kentucky

June 23, 2014: Before I get started on the trip that I had to Waverly Hills, I will once again give a brief history. This history is based off of the history that I found on the Waverly Hills Sanatorium official website.

Brief History: Waverly Hills Sanatorium sits upon land that was originally purchased by a Major Thomas H. Hays in the year 1883. Major Hays needed a school for his daughters to attend, so he began a one room school house located on Pages Lane. He then hired a woman whose name was Lizzie Lee Harris to be a teacher at the school. She loved the school. She also had a fondness for Scott's "Waverley Novels", so much so that it prompted her to name the school "Waverley School." The Major had liked the name and decided to name his property "Waverley Hill." The Board of Tuberculosis Hospital decided to keep the name after they had purchased the land and opened the Sanatorium

Originally Waverly Hills Sanatorium was a two-story frame building. The construction of this building began in the year of 1908 and it opened for business on July 26, 1910. This location was designed to safely house 40-50 tuberculosis patients. At this time tuberculosis was a very serious disease. Those who were afflicted were kept isolated from the general public. They were placed in areas where they could rest and have plenty of fresh air.

Waverly Hills was a self-contained community. A city in and of itself. It had its own zip code. Waverly Hills also had its own post office and water treatment facility. They grew its own fruits and vegetables raised their own meat for slaughter and maintained many of the other necessities for their everyday life. Everyone at Waverly Hills from the patients to the employees had to say 'goodbye' to everything on the outside world. Once in Waverly Hills you would become a permanent resident.

This massive gothic style Sanatorium still remains standing on Waverly Hill today. It could accommodate at least 400 plus patients and was considered one of the most modern and well equipped facilities at the time. In 1962, the building had reopened as WoodHaven Medical Services a geriatric facility. WoodHaven Medical was closed by the state in 1981.

Waverly Hills is now considered one of the most haunted places in the world.

Haunted History: Room 502: Legend says that there was a nurse who found out she was pregnant by the owner of the sanatorium. Without being married and had contracted tuberculosis, she hung herself with a light bulb wire outside the room she was in at the time. Then in 1932 another nurse who worked in Room 502 was said to have jumped from the roof patio, plunging several stories to her death.

The Creeper: On the third floor there are claims of an entity that has been called The Creeper. A black figure that creeps up and down the third floor.

Elevator Shaft: There are tales of a homeless man that was living inside the location both found dead. He and his dog are often seen by the elevator shaft.

Among these few stories there are also claims of shadow people full body apparitions mysterious lights noises and voices.

For more information please visit: www.therealwaverlyhills.c om

I have been waiting to get into Waverly Hills for around seven years now and it did not disappoint. First I had put together a core group, which later would grow, to go to Waverly. It consisted of members from several different local Michigan teams, and of course including Into The AfterLife Paranormal. It took about four hours to get through on the phone to reserve are investigation night. Once it was booked, it was almost unbelievable. After all these years of waiting, I was finally going. I would like to add this, in the week before we were supposed to go, I became very ill. Something was wrong with my leg. It was swollen red and very painful to walk or stand on. I went to the clinic two days to get antibiotics. There was no way that I was missing this trip. I went, my leg got worse and I spent the day after we had got back in the Hospital. I was later told that it was either Cellulitis or Dermatitis, inflammation of the skin, from two different doctors. I am still not sure which it was. It still bugs me to this day.

We pulled up outside the gate early and it was raining that day, so we sat in our cars waiting to enter. A short time later, they opened the gate. Once again that feeling came as we approached the building. The feeling of awe overcame myself. What a sight to see and to finally be there. In fact, I am pretty sure that the feeling was a mutual one throughout all of us that was there. To be honest, it was a bit hectic at the beginning due to the excitement of everyone, but we got through it and began the tour of the location. Another quick note: Some of these encounters that I will write about may seem short, but remember, we had spent very long time there on our sessions and most of that time, as many paranormal investigators can tell you are spent sitting in the dark, waiting.

The Tour

The activity for me started almost from the start. As we entered the building to start the tour, I ended up at the back of the line. The others were headed towards the "Death Tunnel", but something had caught my eye. Down the corridor of the first floor, just pass were we had just entered, I saw a black shadow person standing there. It was pretty far down from us, as if to be watching us from afar, but I could see it and its movement. I began to snap shots off on my camera phone, but caught nothing in the pictures as I headed down towards it. The closer I got, the further back it went and then it was gone. When I caught up to the group, I told Darlene what I had seen. When we reached the roof top, I began to choke and it was very hard for me to breathe. This went on practically the whole time that I was up there. Now was this paranormal? Was I feeling the energy and what the patients with tuberculosis had felt? I cannot say for sure, but it is always a possibility. If this was a sign of the night to come, I could not wait to see what would be next.

The Set Up:

A few of us went up to set up the DVR systems. We decided to put the first system on the second floor and the second on the third floor. We had another system that some other investigators had brought. We used that to mimic some of the cameras on both of the previous DVR setups. As I was planning out some angles on the second floor, I looked over to the stairwell. Up in the upper left corner, as if to be floating, was a shadow person peeking out from behind the wall. I could see what appeared to be a head and shoulders of sort. I watched it for a few seconds. As I took a step forward, it took off. I them remembered what they had told us on the tour. If you see something do not approach it, it will leave. Let it come to you. Which of course makes sense, especially with as many people that come through the location. I am sure that the entities that stay there are more likely to interact on their terms. As I turned from the stairwell, there was a room right there, and standing in the door was another full body shadow person. Was this the same entity or a totally different one I wonder? It once again, was there for a few seconds and then was just gone. I did snap off a few pics, but again nothing was caught. I did go and tell the group that was setting up what I had seen.

Myself and one of my investigators went up to the third floor to start running cameras. The third floor is where "The Creeper" is supposed to be. We stepped out of the room that we were using as the third floor home base. We both stopped dead in our tracks. At the same time, we both had heard what sounded like a deep gravely male voice grunting or possibly clearing its throat. After asking each other what we had heard, we both stood there silently and it happened again. After a while we headed back down to the second floor and once again told the rest of what just happened. We finished the set up and began to start our investigation. We began on the second floor.

Sketch Of the Entity That I Saw On The Staircase

The Second Floor

A small group of us went down to the far end of the second floor corridor. I have to say the frogs on the property were some of the loudest frogs that I have ever heard. Some sounded like they were screaming and the rest sounded like a pack of ravaged monkeys getting ready for a battle. Luckily, they only lasted during the first part of the night. We set up some equipment and began rolling on our digital recorders. The first thing to happen was a noise. A breath to be exact. At least two or three of us heard this. It was a hard deep breath. We acknowledged it at try to figure out what it was. It was suggested that it may had been the EM Pump running, but that is more of a humming sound and later in review of the recording it was definitely a breath, but it is always necessary to check out all possibilities. Shortly after that, I was standing with my back into an open room. Out of nowhere, I heard footsteps walking across the room from behind me. I thought it was one of my investigators. it was that loud to me. I turned and entered the room. To my surprise, there was no other way into or out of the room other than the door that I had been standing in front of. I asked if anyone had heard those footsteps. Some of them said that they had heard something, but I was the only one that heard them as clear as day. After that, we began running the Spirit Box. Now where it did seem like some voices were trying to come through, nothing substantial or clear enough to consider as evidence of an entity. Just as I suggested that we go to the third floor and started to scoop up the equipment, two people came up from another floor and they had some exciting news for me. While doing a session, my last name, Danhausen, came through as they were asking questions. As we finished that conversation and investigator asked if it bothered them that we were here and asking all of these questions, the REM Pod went off. It ran for a bit very strong. We continued to ask questions, but nothing else seems to come through. So after a short time later, we packed up the equipment and headed out to our next location.

The Death Tunnel

We had originally tried to investigate on the third floor at this point, but discovered that there were already investigators there. We did however hear that nobody was in the Death Tunnel. So that is our small group we headed. We entered the area at the top of the tunnel, set up equipment and began. We started off by going down the tunnel individually. The first was one of my investigators. I was second to go. Trekking down was the easy part, although it seemed like there was never going to be a bottom. Coming back up was the hard part. Not only was it hot, but I had been having problems with my leg. Eventually I had made it back to the top. While I was down there, the investigators at the top, including Darlene had heard what sounded like someone entering the area, but nobody ever did. I went down to the entrance area to sit down and rest. I began to see another shadow figure down the hall. It appeared to be coming in and out of the wall. I then heard a knocking on other the wall, but when I tried to re-create it, it did not sound the same. I shouted down to ask if the others had heard it. They were too far away to hear it, but said that that is where they were hearing noises from the tunnel. I then called Darlene down to join me to see if she could see what I was seeing. She could not. At this point we decided to take a break. I headed back, but Darlene wanted to do the tunnel. She headed down by herself. I must say listening back to the recorder, I found her encounters with the bats a bit amusing.

Sketch Of the Death Tunnel Shadow Person

Third And Fourth Floor

After the short break, we decided to head up to the third floor, but for some reason when we reached it, decided to keep going all the way up and work our way down. This however, was a short time investigating. Probably the shortest time that we spent in an area. We proceeded to set up our equipment and the flashlight immediately turned on. Although it would not shut off and I ended up resetting it. So this cannot be used or thought of evidence to me. For a long time we sat quietly in the dark asking minimal questions and making minimal statements. We then began to receive flashlight hits once again, but once again, far too sporadic for me to consider as evidence. I then heard what sounded like rocks being thrown down the hall. No one else had heard this when I asked. Now there was a constant water drip that had been going on the whole time and the noise that I had heard was definitely not the water drip. One of the investigators then began to see a small light at the end of the hall. I had seen this light earlier but thought it was my eyes. As we were investigating, I once again caught a brief glimpse of a shadow person, but as soon as it was there, it was gone. Also, once again, I was the only one to see it. We then decided to head down to the third floor. On a last note for this floor, because it also happened on the third floor. Another encounter for me took place. On both of these floors I kept getting the image of a group of people standing afar at the ends of the halls. It was as if, once again that they were watching us. They seemed content just watching. I did not approach the group as I wanted to see what they would do, but they just watched. Later I had talked briefly to another Medium that was on the trip. She had said that she was getting the same thing. I do wonder though, if it was the same group on both floors. Also at one point, a few of us were watching what appeared to be shadow movement at the opposite end of the hall.

Sketch Of the Group Of Entities In The Halls Of the Third And Fourth Floor

Third Floor

We then move to the third floor. This is supposed to be "The Creeper" floor. We started the session with the Spirit Box. This is when I had seen the group for the second time. They were standing at the end of the hall and I asked if anyone wanted to come forward to speak with us. I saw none of them come forward at that point. I was also hearing nothing coming through the Spirit Box. It was then, that I was then called down to the far end of the corridor by another investigator. She was seeing the laser grid being blocked out. It kept happening to her, but of course once I was down there it had stopped. This is when we decided to go to room 502 located on the fifth floor.

The Fifth Floor

At this point it was getting pretty late into the night. We went up to the roof and set up in the area of Room 502. Out of all the rooms within the Waverly Hills Sanatorium, it is said that room 502 is the most notorious. It is said to have been the area for at least two suicides, including those of a nurse known as Mary Hillenburg, who hung herself in room 502 after becoming pregnant out of wedlock. The second is said to be that of another nurse that jumped out of the window of room 502. After set up, I went out and walked the roof area. Soon after, my camera had malfunctioned. This seemed to have happened several times during this night. I decided to go back into the room and ask some questions. I had received no responses. Some of the group had decided to split up. This sounded like a good way to finish off the night. Myself and Darlene decided to go down to the first floor being how we did not investigate there yet. It seemed that most of the places that we did investigate, we had spent a long time there. So we did not get to as many of the locations in the building that I would have liked to.

The time that we spent on the first floor was short. It was only like twenty minutes. At this point it was very hot, very late and my leg was killing me. Plus, it was getting about that time to tear down the equipment. At this point about half the people had already left and went back to the hotel. I grabbed the remaining investigators that I could find and we got it down. I have to add this in once, again Darlene fell down the stairs screwing up her ankle.

So this will make twice this has happened at two different haunted locations.

So after waiting so long to investigate Waverly Hills, I must say for me it did not disappoint. I do wish however that I would have had more time there to investigate. There is so much area to cover and so little time. Perhaps next year I will be able to make a return trip and cover the areas that I had missed.

Shelby Twp Michigan

July 05 2014: I was contacted about a week after we had got back from Waverly Hills. After about a week worth of frantic calls and texts, I set the date for a small team to go out to the client's location. The client had been seeing these "Faces" throughout their home. I was also told that the dog was being affected. The pictures that I was sent, came across to me as matrixing. I did try to explain this, but the client was quite frantic and was not listening. I was also told that the activity started after she had received a few voodoo doll souvenirs from New Orleans. This is when I decided to take the case, in the least, I would bind the dolls and remove them from the property. Haunted or not, I thought that this may ease the clients mind and in the end help the client out.

We arrived early evening on the Saturday after the Fourth of July. We started our recorders immediately. We also began to run our K2 meters to determine if there were any high EMF's throughout the house. All the time snapping pictures. The client continued to point out these "Faces" to us. Again I tried to explain them away to the client, but it did not seem to take hold. To me though, our job there was to ease the clients mind and help do what we could do. So I told the client that I would bind the dolls and remove them from the property, if that is what was wanted. It was agreed and I began the binding ritual. I used techniques learned throughout my many years of practicing The Craft. I them removed them and we packed up our gear. Hopefully this will work for the client and ease what they believe is happening in the home. For this, only time will tell. If not we will go back and cleanse the home.

Actual Photo: Of The VooDoo Dolls

Livonia Case

Livonia Michigan: 07-18-2014

I received a phone call from the daughter of a woman about her mother, who has been seeing spirits in her home. The home is only around 8 years old, but there are two other factors that may be cause for her activity. First, there is a history of clairvoyance in the family and secondly the home is backed up to a cemetery. Only parted by a chain link fence. I was also told that the husband used to see things as well, but they would just kind of joke it off. Now the mother lives there alone and is seeing the entities for herself. Just from the investigation and speaking with them all, I have a strong belief that she is getting a bleed over from the cemetery. For example, she has never seen the same spirit twice. It is as if they are passing through on their way out and knowing that she can see them, perhaps they are trying to get their final message out. She has witnessed several spirits such as a soldier, a man in a suit, an older woman and a female child. Many of these entities appear to her bedside, which by the way, is a room located closest to the cemetery. It has also been said that the spirit world has an easier time communicating to us when we are asleep. I would suppose that when we are asleep our minds, are uninhibited by our daily thoughts and what we have been taught about ghosts. Our minds are free and able to accept the unlimited possibilities.

We arrived at the home and the whole team, well there was five of us that night, began to interview, not just the homeowner, but the whole family. As I have said before, I do not usually go into a client's home and tell them about what I can see or my personal experiences, but after talking to the mother, I could see that she was very upset with the whole situation. I pulled her aside away from the rest of the family. I then told her that I have experienced the same types of activity that she was not alone. I also explained to her on how she can take control of her home or ask to be shut down from her abilities but what I feel helped her the most was this, I used the soldier entity as an example. I said, I know that it is scary to wake up and see someone standing over your bed, but you must stop and think. This soldier, what did he do in his life? He fought and protected this country and our freedom. I would highly doubt that he would come in here to intentionally scare you and I definitely believe that he would not come here to harm you. As with the rest of the entities. I also explained how I believe that her home is similar to my own, many different entities just passing through.

I finished the talk, including explaining to the client's daughter what I had told her mother and finished helping the team set up the equipment. With such a small group we decided to just stay together. The first session took place in the bedroom. We were not in there long before it hit me. My head started to buzz and my eyes started to water. I then began to fidget my hands as I sometimes do and not realizing that I am doing it. The investigators began tagging my movement. I then realized that I was doing it so I stopped my hands and then my leg started to shake. They then asked me if I was OK I then told them that I was picking up on something. I told them that it started with a group of entities that was gathering at the cemetery fence. Perhaps curious to what we were doing there that night or perhaps wanting to come forward with a message or something. There was one who stood out. An older man in a hospital gown and slippers. He also had frizzy hair. He was at first in the front of the group, then he was mid yard and finally in the room. He stood there for a moment, but said nothing or at least that I could pick up on. Then he was gone. After telling the investigators of what was happening, we decided to move out to the fence.

Sketch Of the Group Of Entities Gathering At The Cemetery Fence

Sketch Of the Old Man In The Bedroom

We reached the fence and began to run the session. There did not seem to be a lot going on out there now, except the bugs biting. So we wrapped it up and headed back inside. I will say this, we did capture, many times, the name Paul throughout the evening. Sometimes in a male voice and sometimes in a female voice, but we will see in review what it may actually mean.

We headed back in and started again in the kitchen. This time we began to get some pretty direct flashlight hits. We continued this for a while. Seeing that the clients in the living room were watching this as well, we decided that we wanted them to take a part in this. So we grabbed up the equipment and moved into the living room. Just a note, the flashlight did not go off again for the rest of the night. Is it because we moved it or maybe there were too many people now, not sure. We began to ask questions and had the clients ask as well. I move to the staircase, which by the way, I had been drawn to since the second I walked into the house. It was the first place that I wanted a DVR camera, even before the interview. As I sat there it began again the feeling. I lay back on the steps and looked above me. Standing there was a younger woman, thin, very pale and brunette. She had no lips, it was a blackness in her eyes and mouth. She had on a pink sun dress on and wearing a pink sun hat. You know one of those big gardening type hats. The name Debbie popped in my head several times. I am not sure if this was her name or not. First time a name has popped in like that. I debated to ask if that was her name and I wanted to ask her about her hat, but I could not decide if I wanted to do it in front of the clients or not. She stood there leaning over me as I was thinking what I wanted to do. It was an odd view for me the way I was laying, she was kind of upside down. By the time I had decided, she was gone. I do tell the investigators later of the woman, but not the clients at this point perhaps on the reveal.

Sketch Of the Young Woman At The Top Of the Stairs

We finished with a short session in a room at the top of the stairs. It was getting late and the clients were getting tired. We wrapped up the equipment and had one final talk with the clients. We let them know that throughout the night, we had been telling whatever was there that when we left that they had to leave. She no longer wanted them in her home. One of our investigators also blessed the home and salted the fence that divided the cemetery from the home. Another investigator also gave the client a blessed rosary. Remember, even though this is not my religious path personally, it is the clients and we will do whatever we can to help them. I am really hoping that along with that, and the long talk that I had with the client, that it helps. Hopefully she can be at peace in her home. If activity continues we shall return and deal with it.

Ypsilanti Michigan

Cleansing : 07-19-2014

The day after the Livonia case, we had a return case to a prior client's home. We had been out there a few months earlier for an investigation. They were really having problems with the entities in their home bothering their children and one of them kept seeing the spirits in the home. We pushed this case to the front. We did go out and although we had caught some evidence, I personally did not feel or see anything. None the less we told them that they needed to move on and that the home owners no longer wanted them there. It seemed to work for a while.

A few months go by and we get in contact with them to see how things are. They proceed to tell us that the activity has returned, but here is why I believe it did. They tell us that they were "messing around" with some phone apps. I really do not like these apps. They are made for fraud and for scaring people. At least that is my opinion. Either way though, by using them, they were still calling something back into the home. We setup to come back out. I was undecided if I wanted to even do an investigation or just the cleansing that the client wanted. When we stepped into the home. It was then that I decided that we were not going to call something in and then cleanse it out. I also told the clients that we would not cleanse if they were going to continue using the apps and calling things in. They informed us that the apps were already deleted. So we went forth with the cleansing.

We first started with one of the investigators speaking to the child that sees the dead. She gave her pointers on how to deal with them and make them go away. After that we began to cleanse. I was documenting the cleansing this time. I had a recorder going, but asking no questions. I was also taking pictures. The rest of the team began to cleanse the home. I had one incident while the cleansing was taking place. Everyone was still in the basement, I stepped into the living room to snap off some pictures. As I entered a dark shadow figure was standing behind the wall by the bathroom. Which by the way, was one of the original claims of activity. We stared at each other for a moment and it took off towards the bathroom. I ran over there and began taking pictures, but caught nothing. I did ask who it was or why it was there. I turned and headed back out to the kitchen. Just before I had left, I caught it again, out of the corner of my eye in the same location. I then left. I did mention this to the team, to let them know to take extra care in this area. We finished the cleansing and headed home. I did listen to the recordings, nothing. Hopefully this will do.

Sketch Of the Back Entity By The Bathroom

A Few Cases Throughout The Years

We have had many more cases throughout the years of investigating. Many of them were private homes and many of them still remain open until this day. I would like to run through some key points on some of them now.

The first case that comes to mind, well was our first case as an official team and our first private home. It took place in Mt Clements Michigan. This case was a very good learning experience for us. Especially for dealing with clients. At first, all was going well. We made contact with the client and set a date. Then the phone calls began. Now let me state this and please don't take me wrong. I know we do this to help the clients and to try and find answers for them and I am glad to do so, but the phone calls were coming multiple times a day. While I was at work, at home and in the late night. I do not mind the clients calling me, in fact I tell them if there is any problems to call me right away, but this started to become excessive. Later on there were other things that we came across that felt odd about the whole situation, which must remain confidential. I got through the calls and the date came to investigate. We ended up investigating two separate times and caught evidence both times. After we had turned over our evidence, we did not here from the client for a while. Then one day, the phone calls started up again. I will not lie, there were thoughts of not going back. This was a very hard client do deal with, but eventually we set a new date. The day before, I got a phone call from the client warning us that his girlfriend may show up to mess with us. I do not know why. I told him that if that was the case, we would reschedule for him to get what he needed in order and then we would come back. I was not going to put my investigators into a situation that they would have to deal with something like that or possibly be put in harm's way. He became very irate and began yelling at me. I then told him that it would probably be better for us to just part ways. He continued with his yelling. I thanked him and wished him the best of luck. He did try calling back about ten minutes later, but I did not answer. I have since been contacted by several different teams that this client has contacted to investigate. So being in the customer service industry for many years, I know how to deal with odd requests and irate people, but in this situation, it had become an extreme situation and showed signs of becoming more of a dangerous one as well. So my best advice if while doing this, if you come across a situation such as this, be polite to the clients, but remove yourselves if you feel off or uncomfortable.

The second case that comes to mind is one that took place in River Rouge Michigan. The key experience at this location was great. Let me lay it out. There were only three of us from the team there that night. We were on our second session now taking place in the basement. We had three separate digital recorders going at different locations throughout the basement. Mine was placed right by the Spirit Box that we had started to run. There was another nearby and one all the way across the room. Now here is the interesting part. We caught a Class A E.V.P. This was only caught on one of the recorders. The one that was placed on the other side of the room. For me, this makes it even more evidence of the paranormal. It also makes it clear that it did not come from the Spirit Box, because the two recorders that were closer to it, never picked it up.

This case came to me from another team and took place in Hazel Park. It started while interviewing the client. Two of us were standing in the dining room talking to the client. All three of us then heard what sounded like a scratching sound on the wall. The three of us all looked over at the same time. I then proceeded to try and replicate the sound. You see the walls had a texture to them to give it a sort of a gravely sound. One scrape of my hand across the surface copied the sound. Later that night we were doing a session the home, it was a smaller home, so we were all spread out we could all see each other. I was sitting at the dining room table and could see down into the kitchen. As I sat there, I kept seeing a black shadow peeking out from behind a tall cupboard that sat on the floor. It kept blocking out the light coming in from the kitchen window. I told the rest of the group, but they never saw it. At that same point, the investigator sitting in the bedroom, which had claims of activity, started to feel uncomfortable. I decided to go sit in there with them. It definitely had a weird vibe to it. It felt off. The investigator left the room and sat in the dining room. Soon after we started to hear knocking sounds. They sounded like they were coming from the closet area which connected to the next room over. This is when I caught an image of a man, it was quick, but I did see him. He was a middle aged man with dark hair and a white shirt. His one distinct feature, his right eye was missing. It was not just missing though, it had looked like it had been eaten away or pecked out by a small animal. We ended up capturing a few E.V.P.'s at this location. Since we have left, the clients say that the activity has calmed down. As a side note, I have noticed that this has happened to several of the client's homes that we have investigated. Once we investigate, the activity seems to subside or leave completely.

Sketch Of the Man That Was Missing His Eye

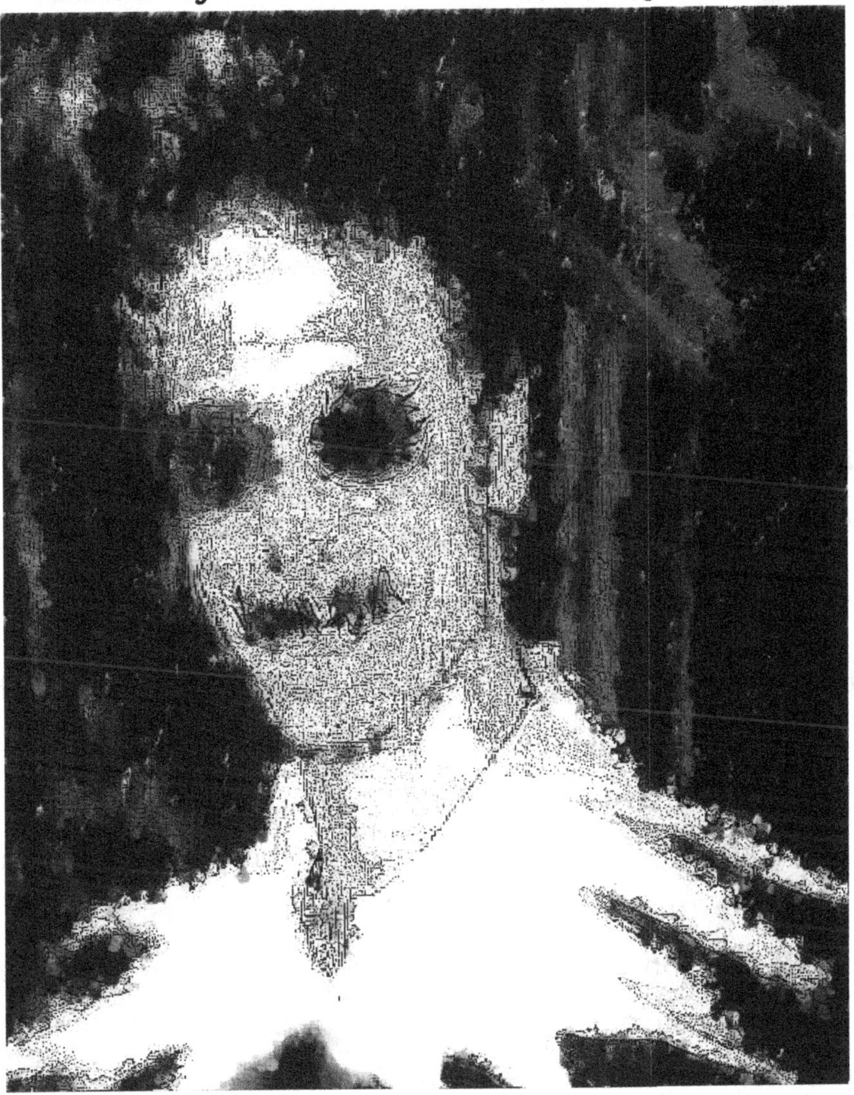

I have to say that meeting with the clients, learning the history of the locations where they live, becoming part of their lives and trying to give them the answers that they seek, well for me it is better than any of the "Bigger" locations that we pay to do the tours on. We have done several homes throughout the years and have caught a lot evidence as well and hopefully help find the answers those clients were seeking. To this day we are still in contact with many of them, as we will stick with our clients throughout the time it takes to make them satisfied and/or feeling safe. I also must add I have been too many locations and have had clients that are not documented in these writings. You see I do not see things everywhere that I go and not everywhere is haunted or has activity.

Other Notable Locations In Michigan That I Have Investigated

The Old Mill in Dundee Michigan

Brief History: The Old Mill it is located along the banks of the River Raisin in Dundee Michigan and is an historic landmark in the Village. Over the years it has served as a grist mill, hydro-electric power plant, Ford factory and fabricating factory. The three-story frame mill was built in 1848-49 by Alfred Wilkerson as a grist mill. The nearby dam had been constructed out of logs in 1846. It is has been restored by community volunteers to create a historical museum. They also now hold haunted tours there.

Haunted History: While there were no documented deaths inside The Old Mill Museum itself, but there are documented deaths at the dam and rumored deaths on the property itself. I myself have seen a photo taken by the team that runs the tour of what appears to be a ghostly hand. I have also witnessed object movement.

For more information please visit www.haunteddundeemill.com

We went to the investigation that takes place at The Mill in Dundee Michigan. This was prior to the team becoming official, but many future members had attended. I personally had some great experiences there. Firs,t the group that I was with had a great dead on flashlight session in the basement. After that, we went around to different locations throughout the mill. I did not have another experience until the end of the night in the banquet hall. This of course is how it always seems to go. Let me explain. It was the last session for me that night. I had my flashlight sitting on a table directly across from us. My 8mm video camera was focused on it. We were there for about a half hour when my tape ran out. I said that being the end of the night that I was not going to get a new tape that I would just run the rest of the session without the camera. A few minutes later, the flashlight which had been sitting there for about 45 minutes, then rolled off the table and fell onto the floor. Of course, no camera on it. We quickly looked around to see if there were any factors that may had caused it. We found nothing. I then went to get a tape and got the camera restarted. Nothing else happened after that. Later while reviewing evidence, I plugged in my digital recorder to my computer. Now I have used this recorder several times, but the second that I plugged it in this time, it began to reformat itself and erased everything that was recorded on it. I had lost any and all potential audio evidence from The Old Mill, among the other files that were on that recorder. I am now in the process of planning a trip back to the mill with the new team members of Into The AfterLife Paranormal.

August 15th/16th 2014: So as it turns out, after I sent the book to be edited, there were some issues with file size due to the amount of pictures. So before I finish resending it in sections, I am able to include my return trip to the Dundee Mill. I think it was meant to be after the events that took place that night.

I arrived at the mill with some ITAP members and some friends and new colleagues. We went on the tour and split into groups. My group headed to the banquet hall. As I walked in, I was about to say sorry for interrupting to the investigator that I thought I saw sitting at the far back table, but as I got closer, I realized that there was nobody sitting there. We began to run a session when we started to hear a loud knocking coming from the room off to the side that we were standing in. We acknowledged it and it did it again. Not sure what it was, but when we asked the people running the event what was above the area, we were told nothing. We stayed a little longer and began to move to the basement.

As we stood at the basement door waiting for the group to come up, we began to get weird K2 hits on two K2 meters. When the group came up they too began to get these hits. It would be there in the middle of nowhere, disappear and not return to the same spot. It was at this time that I saw her. Although I was not on the stairs, I saw the woman dressed in white ascending the basement stairs. She had elongated her face. I believe to try and scare us away. I went to snap some pics on the stairs, but became very hesitant. She made feel very uncomfortable. I snapped one in the doorway and then two down the stairs. Nothing was caught on film though.

The Woman That I saw On The Basement Stairs

It was at this point the K2 hits had stopped and we decided to go into the basement. We sat down by the tanks and set up our equipment. My flashlight was at the far end about 20ft away from us. It came on. It was then asked to be turned off to start a session if they wanted. It did and we began. It was asked if it was the woman that I saw on the stairs, it turned on for yes. It was also asked if she was trying to scare u,s again turned on for yes. There were several other questions asked with direct responses. As we sat there though, I heard what sounded like a breath. The two other people in my group did not hear it though. I began to trance out and started to fidget with my flashlight. The woman was crouched on my right side. It felt as if she was trying to jump me. I had to keep pushing her back. The whole time this was happening the same phrase kept running through my head, "You Do Not Know."

So at that point I snapped out of it, eyes watering and I asked, “What don't we know?" I asked twice and it was at this point I felt a sharp poke on my right shoulder area. It felt like a sharp fingernail. I jumped forward in my chair and said that I think something just poked me. We looked around the area to see if maybe something had fell from the ceiling or perhaps a bug was on me. Nothing was found. I then ask one of the investigators if he would take a look at my back as it was irritating me. He pulled back my vest and shirt and saw two red lines on my back. The other investigator came over to see as well. He then proceeded to take a picture, but his flash was blinding it out. I then handed him my camera and he got the shot although it had started to fade.

We sat down there for a while longer and that was about it until we moved to the elevator shaft. There the K2 began to get weird hits out of nowhere. It soon stopped and we went to the next location.

For the rest of the night I felt pretty at ease. We investigated the rest of the building including outside, but nothing like what had happened in the basement. This is the first time that I have been scratched.

I Am Not Sure How This Picture Will Translate In B&W As When I Put These Pictures In They Are In Color But This Is The Shot Of the Scratch. It Goes Through The Top Of the Moon. Actually As I Was Able To Inspect It Closer You Can See Three Red Lines. It Will End Up On The Website For Better Clarity.

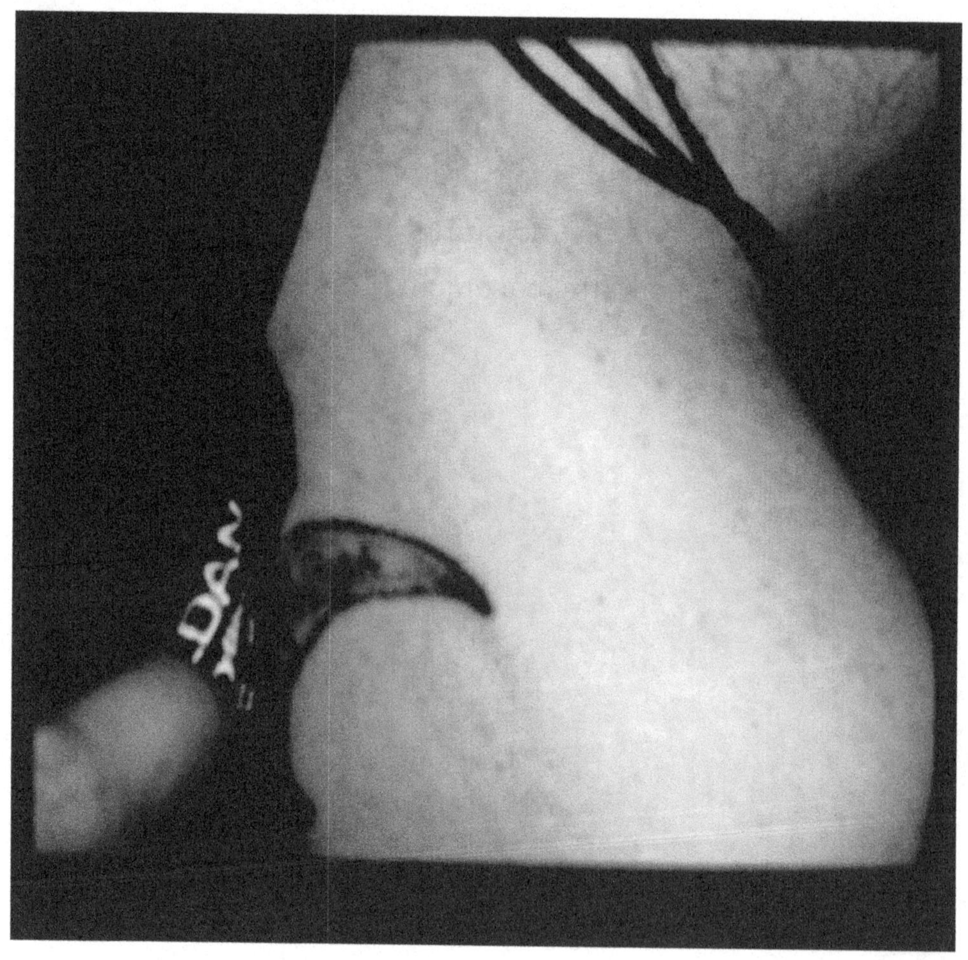

The Allegan Lodge in Allegan Michigan:

Brief History: Although it is often described today as one of the most haunted places in the mid-west, the history of the location begins in 1909 when it was constructed as a hospital for Dr. John Robinson. Very little is known about this era of the building's history, but it is believed that a number of people died at the structure during the time that it was in operation. Which might explain the presence of some of the lingering spirits and paranormal activity that takes place there.

During the 1920's, the rumors also ran rampant that the hospital had ties to organized crime in Chicago and Detroit making the location a convenient spot for the removal of bullets, treating of wounds and a hiding place for injured gangsters. Later, neighbors were said to have spoken of black sedans arriving at the hospital during the night, liquor trucks dropping off shipments of illegal booze and screams that were said to have been sometimes heard in the darkness.

Haunted History: Activity has included cabinets opening in the kitchen, the sounds of children laughing, shadowy figures have been seen in the basement where the morgue was located, conversations have been heard, knocking at the front door and ringing of the doorbell when no one was there, footsteps the sounds of hospital activity and full bodied apparitions of children.

April 7th 2012: This investigation came soon after Into The AfterLife Paranormal was formed. In fact we had just got our first DVR system and this was the first time setting it up and using it. This location, for me, was a great learning experience. Besides the team members we had additional people who attended this investigation with us. I was able to start to learn on how to run the multiple, smaller groups that we break into during investigations. There were some small hiccups of course, but all in all the investigation went great. This, was again, before I had opened myself, but I was still getting the feelings that you get while investigating. We did capture quite a bit of paranormal evidence there and there was one incident that took place that could not be explained. Myself and Darlene went to change tapes in the cameras that were placed in the attic area. Darlene was already getting an uneasy feeling about being in there. As we reached the top of the stairs and were both standing still, we heard a third set of footsteps following us up the staircase. This was not a short brief sound we could hear. The footsteps walk up the full staircase. We immediately started to run the digital recorder and do a small session. In fact, we were the only two in the building at this time. All of the other investigators were outside taking a break. We soon went down and explained what had just happened to the other investigators. When something like this happens, it is very exciting and gets you even more pumped up. During this case, another one of the investigators also had personal experience. I was not there, but the investigator told us of getting pushed on her way out of the kitchen while entering the ball room. We also had some direct flashlight responses and K2 hits and as written before, the experience that took place in my home after the investigation.

The Yale Hotel Yale Michigan:

A Brief History: For some reason it was really hard to find anything on this location for me, but The Yale Hotel is a 110 year old historical working hotel and restaurant.

Darlene and I were invite by our team member and friend Candace to an overnight ghost hunt taking place at the hotel. They had a cancellation and an opening came up. The event was being hosted by a local team. This was the first time that I had actually heard of this location. I was really looking forward to it. We approached the location. It is an older building with a working bar/ restaurant on the ground floor. Once the bar shut down, we were able to begin. It started with group tour and sessions throughout. We were then left to investigate on our own. We went for a while, but Darlene and I became tired very fast. We had both worked that day and have been up since early morning. Although, some of the others there had some Spirit Box and K2 hits and I felt a presence watching us from the hall as we did our first group session, I did not capture any evidence for myself. The building is certainly worth another trip out to investigate.

Life Death and Rebirth of a Paranormal Team

Let start this section by saying as above, that if you are thinking of entering this field for financial gain or to get on a T.V. show you are entering for the wrong reasons. Sure, once in a great while something like that may happen as we all can see from the shows that we all watch, but I would not count on it. We do this because it is something we love. To help both ourselves and our clients. To find answers to our questions. It is like I always said while working in the haunted attraction field, if this is something that you would not do for free, than you probably should not be doing it. This is a job a non-paying job, but a job none the less. When you accept clients, you are now working for them, they are there for your help and you are there to do so. Once I had accepted this, things went much, much better. You must be committed. This is a very time consuming field to be in. More so if you do decide to take on clients. If you decide just to go on the public type investigations, which is fine as well, it will be a little less of a commitment. You can run on your own time line as opposed to the clients. So be committed and be prepared and do it, because it is something that you love and are passionate about. With that being said, I am going to end this book with the story of the ups and downs of having and creating a paranormal team. Some people may think that it may be easy, but let me tell you that it is not. In fact it is far from it. I had spent months and months researching names alone before even starting the team, among other things such as rules and regulations, waivers, websites, how to deal with clients and equipment. At points, I would find myself completely consumed by it. So much so, that at times it has affected my family life. Although the more I push forward and the more that I learn and grow, I am now starting to find it easier to step back when I need to and focus more on my life outside of the paranormal.

So let start at the beginning. As I said above, you must start by researching a lot of things before you can even begin to put a team together. There are a lot of paranormal teams out there, worldwide in fact. So finding a name that is not already taken is time consuming and frustrating in itself. Just when you think that you may have one, your search reveals that you do not. You must also put together a rules and regulation form for your investigators and waivers for your clients. If you choose to take on client cases as opposed to just going on the bigger paid locations. If you are going to be dealing with clients, you may want to think about a website for easier contact. They will also want to be able to see what you and your team is all about before letting you into their home. Again, a website is perfect for this. So I do suggest some strong research before jumping into anything paranormal or not.

After I finished my months of research, but keep in mind that all the while I had been also investigating at the bigger more famous locations learning along the way. Once I had all in place for my team Into The AfterLife Paranormal, I approached my wife Darlene about running and finding the team with me. She had suggested that maybe I should approach my brother about helping me run it. To make it a family thing. I thought that it was a great idea. Let me give you a brief background on the brother situation. We both had different mothers and would see each other every other weekend at our fathers when we were very young. That ended and I had not seen him again for many, many years later. I would then see him from time to time, but mostly just in passing. Some tragic events had taken place in the family and we had begun talking. Both the families were into the paranormal and have been dealing with it for a while. So when I approached him it was a go for all of us, the two brothers and our wives.

So my research was done, the website up and running and all was in place. So the next step was bringing in investigators. Me and Darlene were investigating with a few ladies from my work, so that was a good place to start. From there I knew a few others linked through my work that had gone on prior investigations with us and/or that were interested in the paranormal field. I brought their names to the leaders and after discussing it and we invited them in. Now with the team in place it was time to start investigating.

Our first case came surprisingly fast. It was a private home in Clinton Township Michigan. We also all worked together well. Don't get me wrong, it took us a while to get into our groove, but for our first private residence it went really smooth. We actually ended up back at this location several times. Which leads me to mention this real quick. Usually we will stay with a client until the end. One time out does not usually close a case, but occasionally, a client may become too much to handle. Calling multiple times a day for weeks on end. They do not understand that while we are there to help many of us in this field have families, jobs and lives outside the paranormal. Sometimes you may find yourself cutting ties with a certain client. It is a hard choice to make, but sometimes it is for the best and must be done.

So let's jump ahead a bit. We had a lot of investigations during the time that the original team was together and had many paranormal experiences. We also caught a great deal of evidence and to this day, I will still say that they are all great paranormal investigators. It went really well for about a year and a half. Then something happened and it began to fall apart. A separation between members started to form. You also started to see groups form within the group. It was no longer starting to feel like a team. A few of the investigators then decided to leave. On a side note, I still talk to them. I would never not speak to someone just because they left the team. It was just not for them anymore. Not the path that they were looking for. You could feel the tensions building within the group for several months. It seemed though that if it was ever asked about or brought up, it got pushed away and everything was always said to be fine. Let me say that I know that all teams have their bumps and stops along the way and I understand that you go through these and grow, but this was not happening here. Things just kept getting worse. Now I also understand that things happen and nobody is perfect. Especially myself. We were all new at this and had to learn together, the good and the bad. In fact, even when there was only myself and my wife left on the team or with the new team that are currently in the fold, I am still learning and always will be.

Eventually the split happened. I will not go into the gruesome details of the split. As I have said and will always say whatever happened between the original members, shall stay among the original members or at least it will not come from me. The split had cost me enough already. In the end, the remaining members left and formed their own team leaving only me and my wife Darlene with Into The AfterLife Paranormal. Now of course I was not happy about the way that it had ended. I do not think that anyone was, but I cannot or do not wish to try and change the way other people had felt. They had done what they wanted to do and that is that. They wanted to take a different path I suppose. I have accepted it a long time ago and have moved passed it and also whatever some of them may believe I had wished them all the best of luck. They were after all my family. Even the ones who were not blood were still family. That is the most tragic part of the split. It was not losing the team. I had always said that if anyone ever decided to leave the team, that we would wish them the best of luck and remain friends, but losing my family in the process, that is what crushed me. Even though it had ended badly, we had many, many great times and memories together and hopefully someday all of this will pass and we will be able to be family again. I still talk to several of the old team members from time to time.

So we live and we learn and we must move forward. After the bad times of the split. a great unity began to develop in the paranormal teams in Michigan. I liked the feeling of this teams meshing together, sharing investigations and evidence, helping each other. This was the path that I wanted to take the team in. It was the start of the path that Into The AfterLife Paranormal was going to head on. No more drama, no more tensions within a team. Even though there was only two of us left, the support from the community was incredible. We were invited by other teams to join in on their investigations and take part in their different events that they may have had going one. We felt like a part of something bigger than we had in a very long time and I would like to take a second on behalf of myself and Darlene to thank all of you that had helped us out through the rough times. It was greatly appreciated and we love you all. You all know who you are. So I took these new feelings and the greatness that I felt from all of the other the teams and decided to put it into forming the new team. This time though I was going to take my time and really put even more thought into it than I had done before.

I began receiving requests to join the team almost immediately, and so I decided to start and rebuild. I had started to conduct the interviews and what I ended up with, was that I could not ask for better team mates. All of the new members that I have brought in could not be more professional, caring people. Whether they have years of experience or have just recently started in the paranormal field, they all have given their all thus far and I couldn't be prouder of what they all have brought to Into The AfterLife Paranormal. I also know, and we have already had a few minor bumps in the road, and I am sure that there will be more, but we now leave it all on the table. If there is a problem, it is confronted head on, resolve and learn from it and then we all move forward. Now I do believe that everything happens for a reason and since I have started to rebuild, great things have been happening. I have had more experiences, met more new people, worked with many great teams and have become a part of something much bigger than I ever thought I would have, and it still keeps coming. I cannot wait to see what else the future holds. If the events of recent times is any indication, then I am in for one Hell of a great ride

Paranormal Unity

So as I said above, around the time of the original teams parted, a great unity was forming throughout the paranormal teams in Michigan. We were friends with several of the teams already, but this was turning into something much larger. For me it started when I made an open forum page on a social media site ironically called Into The AfterLife: Paranormal World. This was a place that I had made so that anyone interested in the paranormal could come and ask questions, tell their stories or even promote their events. Unfortunately, I became swamped with cases, among other things and was not able to push it the way that I wanted to. The page still exists and is now building.

There is also a Paranormal Picnic that had started. It was started by the team S.W.P.I. They also run the investigations out in Dundee Michigan. A lot of the teams will get together and of course eat, but all communicate with each other exchanging ideas and theories.

After that, I was at a huge paranormal convention up in the Upper Peninsula. There I began talking to a friend Mark and

Terri from another local team, Marter Paranormal. He began to tell be of a group that he had started called The Michigan Paranormal Association, the MPA. This is a group of teams that all work together. For an example, if I had a case and all of my investigators became ill or whatever and they could not make it, I can post that to the MPA site that I need help and MPA members will help me. It may be several different members from several different teams, but the help will be there. This goes for any member of the MPA. We also can post evidence and get other teams opinions on it. Even if we just want to run theories by each other. Well once I had heard this, I wanted in. This is the direction that I wanted Into The AfterLife Paranormal to go in. We are now getting ready for a huge event on May 31st 2014, the Michigan Paranormal Gathering in Bath Michigan. Although the teams of the MPA will be running this event, all teams are welcome to set up and anyone interested in the paranormal are invited to this totally free event. They can come out to meet the local teams ask questions or whatever. Hopefully if all goes as planned, this will become a yearly event. So we would like to thank Mark and everyone in the MPA for making us a part of all of this. It is a fantastic group to be a part of.

May 31st 2014: The Paranormal Gathering in Bath Michigan. Again, I would like to give you all some background for the area where the gathering took place. Although I have never personally investigated this area, I hear it is quite haunted. This information comes directly from the memorial plaque that is placed in the park.

On May 18th 1927, a dynamite blast rocked the Bath Consolidated School shattering one wing of the building and resulting in the deaths of thirty-nine children and teachers ; dozens more were injured. An Inquest concluded that dynamite had been planted in the basement of the school by Andrew Kehoe, an embittered school board member. Resentful of higher taxes imposed for the schools construction and the impending foreclosure on his farm, he took revenge on Bath's citizens by targeting their children. Soon after the explosion, as parents and rescue workers searched through the rubble for children, Kehoe took his life and the lives of four bystanders including the superintendent one student and two townspeople by detonating dynamite in his pick-up truck as he sat parked in front of the school.

I have to say, standing on the location were this took place, reading the plaque, well I could almost picture it in my mind and what all of those people had gone through. It sent chills up and down my spine.

The gathering once again brought many local Michigan teams together, although many were MPA members, many other teams attended as well. We also got to meet new teams and people and others who just came to meet us and ask questions or share stories. The whole gathering was a great success. That night I had the dream that I earlier in the "My Current Residence" section.

After we had joined the MPA, another site popped up on the social media. The Paranormal Unity Center. This was create by another person from a local team, Downriver Paranormal and friend from Michigan, Ryan. This page took off quickly. It was again a place for all to come together and share ideas and information open to all not just teams. Thank you Ryan for putting that page together. It has brought a lot of attention the cause.

Another great moment of unity for me, happened after the break of the team. It was just I and Darlene, we of course were feeling down. I was contacted by a friend Candace, who would later join Into The AfterLife Paranormal, but at the time was the Director of Beyond The Veil Investigations. She had invited us to join them on an investigation, along with some other friends from another team. I was excited, this was the first investigation that I was going on since the break of the team and it was at a local haunted attraction that had claims of being haunted. So for me, after being in a slump, was great. It was a great investigation and we had an awesome time. I was soon asked by Candace again, to join them on another investigation. This was at the Historical House located in

Royal Oak Michigan. So again, I would like to thank Candace and everyone at Beyond The Veil Investigations for helping me out of my slump and for letting us be a part of their story. I would also like to thank Lisa from Third Eye Paranormal Society. Her group sent a few cases our way and we were grateful to have them.

Next, I would like to mention another group of people who have always showed unity to every team. Metro Paranormal Investigations, MPI. This is the group, among other things, ran The Fort Tours in Detroit. Since I have first met this group, they have been more than friendly to us. They have always answered my questions about the field and the paranormal without hesitation, and I have asked a lot. Throughout the years they have become very good friends. Myself and Darlene even have become a part of their crew on the radio show that they do, The Chris and Wayne Show. This is a paranormal radio show. It takes place aboard "The Haunted Ship Of Doom", where Darlene and myself have become known as "The Stow Aways." The last time that we went down to The Fort, we went down to help them out as volunteers and had a great time with them. I would like to thank them for all for the support that they have shown us and Into The AfterLife Paranormal, among others in the community as well. They are always there to help who needs it and I am glad they we have met this group of individuals and become friends. Thank you to Chris, Wayne, Wendy, Deana, Jo, Russ, Kristie, Kevin, Jan and Mikey. I need to give a special thanks to Mike and Stephanie. Me and Darlene have had a blast on the investigations that we have went on with you guys and we are looking forward to many more. We always have a great adventure with you two. If I forgot anyone in MPI, I apologize.

As I am thanking people I would also like to thank, Anna and Jerry who run a local shop in WoodHaven Michigan, The Smokey Crystal LLC. They gave us our first meet and greet at their store, which led to our first tour. They were having a cemetery tour and had asked us to help run it. So we did. We had a fairly large group of people that night and even though it had rained the whole time, everyone had enjoyed it especially us.

Another thanks must go out to Corvis and Dark Moon Press for giving me the opportunity to shares my experiences and thoughts with you all.

Also, a thanks to those that I may have missed. I have met a lot of great people and teams throughout these paranormal years. A big thanks to the new team as well. We have come together as a team very fast and work together well.

Thank you to the members of Into The AfterLife Paranormal, thank you all for putting up with me and my ways. You guys are all great and I am very proud of all of you and the work that you all have done and continue to do.

A special thanks goes out to my good friend Keri, without you, I would not be as far as I am at in the paranormal field. It was you who had rekindled my fire for it, all those years ago

Finally, a huge thank you to my family who has supported me through all of this. It has been a long and bumpy journey thus far and they have stuck by me through it all. I know that they will continue, because even though this has been almost a lifetime in the making, I know that this journey is far from over.

On my final note, I would just like to say that there have been many rough times in this life dealing with the paranormal, but there has also been some very good times and with anything in life, you will have to take the good with the bad. And so the clients are still booking dates and we are still booking our larger trips and planning future tours among other things. I have since gained a better control and understanding when dealing with the dead and have learned a lot from not only myself, but a great deal of friends and colleagues. I am looking forward to the future and what it holds for myself and the paranormal field.

Thank You

Types of Hauntings

I found these descriptions of hauntings, throughout the years from the internet. They give a very good description on the different types of hauntings and I wanted to share them

Traditional Hauntings:

This type of haunting is probably the most accepted type of haunting but is not as common as you might think.

This type of haunting involves a ghost or ghosts that are intelligent or interactive. This means that they can interact with this world and are aware when people are around and what is going on around them. They may respond to someone who is trying to communicate with them or maybe even try to appear to them. These types of hauntings are *usually* connected with a location or a person that is at that location.

The interactive ghost is the consciousness of the person that once lived. This means that it has all the knowledge, personality and habits of that person. This person may have decided to stay behind instead of moving on, or because of murder, an accidental death, unfinished business, an undying love for someone or many other reasons.

Because of the fact that the ghost retains all of the emotions and personality of the living person it once was, there is the potential for there to be benevolent, *peaceful spirits*, as well as malevolent, *angry spirits*. Please do not confuse malevolent spirits with an inhuman entity a malevolent spirit was once human and may just give off an angry feel in the air and possible tension and animosity around the area that it is haunting. These negative spirits are not *evil* but angry. This may be due to their confusion and unsure of what is going on around them. This also may mean that in life they may have been an angry person and that it carried over into their death.

Residual Hauntings:

This type of haunting is like watching a movie play over and over again. These hauntings are cause by an energy that has been imprinted on a particular location. These hauntings occur when a major event takes place at a location and the psychic memory of that event is left behind after those people are gone. That does not have to mean that they died in some cases the people are still alive but the event was so dramatic that it still left its imprint. Many times these hauntings are said to have sounds, smells as well as apparition sightings. The difference between *Traditional Hauntings* and *Residual Hauntings* is that the ghost in a residual haunting is not responsive. You can talk to it and it would not answer you. It is just replaying events long passed. Even though they do not acknowledge you, you can still pick up evidence from them on your equipment such as E.V.P.'s and photographs etc.

Poltergeist Hauntings:

Thanks to Hollywood, the word *Poltergeist* is a household word. While the movies are entertaining they *do not* show a true poltergeist type of haunting. Poltergeist comes from the German word meaning "noisy ghost", a poltergeist is centered around a person, usually called an agent. While poltergeist activity can take place with any agent, it has been known more to take place with adolescent girls during their puberty stage of life.

Poltergeist activity is associated with objects being move and thrown as well as footsteps and rapping sounds. While these sounds may be similar to the activity of the two previous types of hauntings, the activity is coming from a person and not a ghost. The agent is actually causing the events to happen unknowingly. The agent has emotions held inside due to stress and other aggravating factors. The agent has no way of expressing these emotions so they lash out psychically through the events found in a poltergeist type haunting. When investigating a poltergeist case, there may be no scientific evidence to be found in the form of EVP, EM readings and photographic. That is because there is no ghost. The way to determine this type of haunting is to remove the possible agent from the location and see if the activity continues.

This activity is usually short term, ranging from a few weeks to as long as a few years. Counseling for the agent will often help if not extinguish the activity all together.

Inhuman Hauntings:

This type of haunting is not very common. Inhuman hauntings are almost always malevolent beings. The difference between ghostly hauntings and inhuman hauntings is that the name says it all. The entity was never human. These hauntings fall under a “Demonic" category. These hauntings may in fact coincide with *possession*. Anyone who ever has encountered one of these beings can tell you that it is not a pleasant experience. These usually have to be dealt with on a much higher level such as having *spiritual* leaders come and assist in banishing the entity. This can be a long and grueling ordeal.

Glossary

ANOMALY: An irregular or unusual event which does not fit a standard rule or law. An anomaly is something which cannot be explained by currently accepted scientific theories. Anything weird, abnormal, strange, odd, or difficult to classify is considered an anomaly.

AUTOMATIC WRITING or **AUTOMATIC ART:** To freely channel your higher self or another soul's words, music, or art without the interruptive interference of the mind.

AVP (Audible Voice Phenomena): the disembodied voices that are heard at the time of the investigation and may or may not be recorded on electronic devices.

CLAIRAUDIENCE: Hearing voices, astral music or discarnate beings.

CLAIROLEOFACTOR: To have an extraordinary sense of smell, as if you could smell flowers before they bloom or smell trouble before it occurs or death before it happens.

CLAIRSENTIENCE: The ability to clearly feel yours and/or another's emotions. One who studies and practices the art of demonology. An individual who specializes in the removal of evil or demonic forces from a given environment using the art of demonology. One who brings demonic forces out of their slumber to be cast away. Someone who uses the art of demonology to incarnate demons for one's use in battling them and sensations.

CLAIRVOYANCE: To have lucid mental perceptions and keen insights about people and life situations and to have clear visual mental images, pictures, to "see" auras and other psychic phenomena.

DEJÀ VU: Certain events and experiences seem as if you are re-experiencing the event or situation that has happened at another time. As familiar as the experiences are, you cannot recall nor figure out when they happened.

DIRECT WRITING: Direct writing is when spirits actually write using any means. This can be done by slate writing or by pen and paper.

DIVINATION: The ability to obtain unknown knowledge of future events from omens. Astrology may be considered divination.

DIVINING ROD: A forked rod from a tree said to indicate the presence of water or minerals underground.

DOPPELGANGER: A spirit of a living person outside of the physical body.

DOWSING ROD: Simple tool of metal or wood used to locate water, lost objects, energy fields or in spirit communication.

Established use has been known for centuries but carries little or no weight within current scientific arenas.

ELECTROMAGNETIC FIELD (EMF): Energy field surrounding all things, both natural and man-made.

ELEMENTALS: Term commonly referring to natural spirits. AKA "Earth spirits".

ENTITY: Anything that has a separate, distinct existence, though not necessarily material in nature.

ELECTRONIC VOICE PHENOMENA (EVP): sounds found on electronic recordings which resemble speech, but are not the result of intentional recording or rendering. EVP are commonly found in recordings with static, stray radio transmissions, and background noise. Recordings of EVP are often produced by increasing the gain (i.e. sensitivity) of the recording equipment.

EMPATHY: Rarely used in modern parapsychology, the popular usage of this term refers to a low-level form of telepathy wherein the empath appears to be aware of the emotional state of a distant person. An empath may also be able to "broadcast" emotions to others.

ESP: Extrasensory perception (ESP) is the knowledge of external objects or events without the aid of the senses.

EXORCISM: The banishment of an entity or entities (spirits, ghosts, demons) that are thought to possess or haunt a location or human being or animal. The ritual, which can be religious in nature, is conducted by an exorcist who will call upon a Higher Power to cast away any evil forces that may be present.

INFRA-RED CAMERA (IR Camera): Camera with incorporated infra-red technology that allows photography or filming in low light conditions. AKA "night vision camera.

INNER VOICE: Receiving guidance and assistance from inside of you.

INTUITION: Act of knowing without the use of usual rational processes. Based partly on subconscious pattern association of known information, and partly on subconscious psi impressions.

MAGNETOMETER (EMF meter, Gaussmeter, K2): Instrument for measuring the magnitude and direction of a magnetic field; typically used by paranormal researchers to detect a ghost's magnetic energy.

MEDIUM: Someone who professes to be able communicate with spirits on behalf of another living being, acting as a midway point halfway between the worlds of the living and the dead.

OUIJA BOARD: A pre-printed board with letters, numerals, and words used to receive spirit communications. Typically a planchette, a triangular or heart-shaped pointer, is employed to spell out words or messages and point out numbers or letters. Many believe the controversial board is a gateway allowing negative entities into the physical plane while others believe it no more harmful than any other board game. AKA "spirit board", "talking board". The board's name is derived from the French and German words for 'yes'.

OUT-OF-BODY EXPERIENCE or **ASTRAL PROJECTION**: To be able to leave your physical body and project your soul, consciousness or what appears to be your mind to another place and return via a silver cord.

PAST LIFE RECALL: To remember or have mental flashes about living in another century.

POLTERGEIST: A general term applied to a variety of site-, or sometimes person-, specific physical phenomena. These can include temperature variations, anomalous sounds, and movement of physical objects. The word 'poltergeist' literally means 'noisy spirit' and was coined back when such phenomena were thought to be due to the presence of some sort of mischievous entity. Currently, poltergeist phenomena are usually considered to be related either to unusual physical conditions at the affected site, or to be related to psychokinesis. Anecdotal reports suggest that many poltergeist focus on an individual under some form of emotional stress.

PRECOGNITION: Pre-knowing; where nondeductible information about a future event is acquired.

PRECOGNITIVE DREAMS: To have dreams of events or incidents before they happen.

PREDICTION: To be able to predict future events before they occur.

PSI: A general term for parapsychological phenomena that includes informational (RV, ESP) and energetic (PK) effects. Psi, or Y, is the 23rd letter of the Greek alphabet.

PSYCHIC: Popular term used to denote a person who regularly uses, or who appears to be especially gifted with, psi abilities. Also refers to general phenomena related to the mind (from Greek *psyche*).

TELEKINESIS, PSYCHOKINESIS, LEVITATION: To move an object or your body without physical means.

TELEPATHY: To know what others are thinking as if to hear thoughts in your head. Thought transference including the sending and receiving of thoughts.

RANSMEDIUMSHIP, TRANSCHANNELING: To have severe ›ersonality shifts.

VORTEX: An anomaly that appears as a funnel or rope-like image in photographs. Sometimes thought to represent ghosts, collections of orbs or gateways which travel to a wormhole in time-space, there is no substantial scientific evidence to support any of these theories.

WHITE NOISE: An acoustical or electrical noise of which the intensity is the same at all frequencies within a given band.

Made in the USA
Middletown, DE
09 May 2024

54011091R00156